PRACTICAL
NOVEL WRITING

This book is dedicated to the memory of my father, author of the widely-unpublished crime novel THE WILLOWS WEPT, who offered assistance right from the start when, aged 8 (approximately), I began struggling with my own early works – BY UMBRELLA TO THE MOON and BEAUTY THE PONY (original mss sadly abandoned and or lost)

with belated thanks and love

Natasha, the Beautiful Spy

THE WRITERS NEWS LIBRARY OF WRITING

Other volumes in preparation

PRACTICAL
NOVEL WRITING

Dilys Gater

DStJT
WN

'And what are you reading, Miss – ?'
'Oh! it is only a novel!' ... or, in short, only some work in which the most thorough knowledge of human nature, the happiest delineation of its varieties, the liveliest effusions of wit and humour are conveyed to the world in the best chosen language.'

Jane Austen – Northanger Abbey

ISBN 0 946537 70 4

A catalogue record for this book is available from the British Library

Set in 11/12.5pt Sabon by XL Publishing Services
Printed in Great Britain by
Billing & Sons Ltd, Worcester
for David St John Publishers
PO Box 4, Nairn, Scotland IV12 4HU

CONTENTS

PART III THE PROFESSIONAL TOUCH
Preparation, Presentation and Submission of your Novel

PART IV   THE GENRE NOVEL

PART V   WHAT MAKES A BESTSELLER?

PART VI AUTHOR'S NOTE

INTRODUCTION

ANYONE can write a novel. This is a fact, not a fallacy. Anyone at all can shut himself away with his typewriter or word processor, and cover sheets of paper or discs with a narrative he claims is his great work, his 'novel'. But most novels written in this way are unsuccessful, and the authors never know why. The purpose of this book is to help you, the reader, to write a *good* novel which will also be a *successful* novel, as opposed to the amateurish, unreadable and unsaleable material which many would-be novelists fret over for years, and then have to abandon in despair because no publisher will touch it.

So first, a few dos and don'ts to clear the ground before the actual work begins.

1. Consider your motive. Why do you want to write a novel? It is not a good idea to attempt one because you want to make money quickly, or enhance your reputation, or because all the novels you have read are rubbish and you want to show the authors how to write. The only really valid reason for wanting to write a novel is because you cannot possibly *not* write it, and you will not be able to rest if you don't get it out of your system.

2. Do not use your novel in order to air any theories you might have on subjects which would be better suited to a non-fiction book. Theories are not fiction.

3. Don't try to describe some true happening or event in your novel, detailing it at great length because 'this is how it was'. Fiction is an art form, and the whole structure of a novel has to be highly unrealistic and artificial for it to work successfully.

7

4. Many first novels – or even second or third ones – are written in an attempt to capture the past or externalise long-ago traumas in the writer's life. Make sure this is not at the back of your own desire to write, for laying your own particular ghosts to rest in your work, without proper consideration of the novel form and its requiremants, will probably be very therapeutic and make you feel much better but will not result in good literature.

5. Bear in mind that you are writing your novel *now*, rather than yesterday, ten or even twenty years ago. Envisage your readers as people of today or of five or ten years in the future, and do not write for society as it was when you were in your teens or twenties. Try not to allow your book to be 'dated' either in its style of writing or in the way you tackle your subject matter.

6. It is surprising how often new writers include within their first novels the skeletons of at least six books. Do not try to cover every variation of subject that occurs to you, nor explore every interesting thought which strays into your mind. You will only need to keep something in reserve for the next book you write.

7. However tempting it is, do not write about things which are alien to your experience or run contrary to your own beliefs. If you simply cannot imagine how any woman could ever stray from her dull, boring but infinitely dear husband, don't feel obliged to be 'modern' and include an affair or two for your liberated heroine before she settles for home life for good and all, having had her fling. Nobody can write convincingly about anything he cannot, in his secret heart, comprehend or believe in.

A novel is good if it works successfully within the limits of the writer's experience and capabilities and his sincere attempt to incorporate true values, as he conceives them, into his writing. Falsity, 'talking-down', tongue-in-cheek work will all nullify any other qualities a novel might have. It may seem very gripping, but without something in it of the writer's own awareness of truth, with which a reader can identify, it will be empty and will soon bore anyone who tries to read it.

The author's truths may be only superficial, possibly even shallow, but if they are genuine the novel will contain something good. We cannot all have the immense sweeping vision of genius, but every sincere and honest writer who writes a novel to *the best of his ability* can feel, in however modest a way, that he has done a good job.

PART I
BASIC GROUNDWORK

1
CHARACTERS

A T its most basic level, a novel is an account of the feelings, thoughts and events befalling a group of nonexistent people. These people are your characters. There can be no novel without characters, whether they are human beings, animals or even creatures from another galaxy arriving on Earth when the human race has destroyed itself.

The characters are the actors in the story you have to tell; they provide the conflict which will arouse the reader's interest and keep him guessing as to the outcome, and they give the story movement which carries it forward. A story with no characters wouldn't be a story, it would be a descriptive passage about the scenery, or some sort of essay about what the author thought on a certain subject. A novel needs to be about characters the reader can believe in, people with whom he can identify, who seem real and human and whose eventual fate will become of paramount importance to him as the novel progresses.

How do you dream up your characters?

Nobody can answer this question directly for you. If I actually described characters you could use in a book, those would be characters I had created and would not be your own. Indirectly, however, there are many methods you can use to help you to find the characters who are going to make your book memorable.

Some writers try to capture people they know, rather in the manner of hunters armed with large nets to bring home the 'big game'. They attempt to transfer their characters as faithfully as possible from real life into the pages of their novel. This very seldom works because, as has already been briefly mentioned, a novel, like a painting or a piece of music, is an art form, and though it might look like real life, it is actually artificial.

A novel – indeed all fiction – is *based on* real life. Characters in a novel have to be *based on* real people, to some extent, but a writer who attempts to transfer a real person directly from life onto the typewritten page is trying to do the impossible.

It is much better to take bits and pieces of various people you might know, and many novelists do this quite unconsciously. A writer can only draw on the experiences and knowledge within his own mind; all his characters will be a product of these, overlaid with habits, idiosyncracies, physical characteristics that have somehow strayed in from recollections of other people he has stored up over the years.

As you work on your own characters, you too will do this; but it is the actual starting point that worries most new writers, the creation of the people who are going to act out the novel.

HINTS TO HELP YOU CREATE CHARACTERS

1. It often gives you something to hang on to if you look through old magazines (or even new ones) for pictures of faces. Books containing reproductions of paintings can work just as well. One face will suddenly stand out and you will know immediately that you've got your heroine, or your hero.

It is better for this purpose if you do not really know who the faces belong to – for instance, if the magazine is written in a language you don't understand. The face is all you need; your imagination will give you the rest of the details about your character, and it can be very off-putting if, having seen the mysterious high cheekbones and haunting eyes of your novel's beautiful but tragic central character, you happen to read in the caption below that the face actually belongs to Tracy Higgins, a butcher's assistant from Clapham who has just won a local beauty contest and a week for two in sunny Spain.

Imagination works best if it is starved of facts. Once

Tracy Higgins has laid claim to that haunting and mysterious face, it will never seem the same and you have lost your heroine. Cut out the pictures of faces (or get someone else to do it for you) so that there are no identifying marks, names or captions as you look through them. Keep a collection, so that whenever you want to bring in a new character and you just cannot seem to 'see' him or her, you only need to spend an hour with your faces and you've got what you want.

One novelist who used this idea not to create her characters but to start off her novel – and whose writing illustrates the way imagination will work overtime when confronted by just a face – was Josephine Tey in her excellent *The Daughter of Time*. Read this as an example of a novel 'twist' being given to what might have otherwise been a straightforward report of historical research. The way in which her contemporary detective 're-creates' the characters of the past offers a lesson for beginner writers on how to approach creating your characters, by a recognised story-teller and skilled mistress of her craft.

2. Study people everywhere you go, on buses, trains, in shops, supermarkets. Details will stay in your mind and come back to you as you rack your brains for new characters. As with the face pictures, people you do not know are best. A tired figure, stooping a little to the right; that man with the golden tan, the thick blonde hair, the expensive clothes – he seemed like a Greek god. Until you saw his eyes. The way one girl holds her head; a child reaching out with no sense of fear to a vicious-looking dog twice its own size. Take notice of all these things. Watch, observe. As Christopher Isherwood put it: 'I am a camera with its shutter open, quite passive, recording, not thinking.'

It has been said that the role of the novelist is that of a voyeur. This is to a certain degree true. You cannot be a good novelist – or even an averagely competent novelist – without using your senses keenly everywhere you go and storing up details, impressions and sensations. The novelist's private life is often (to the uninitiated) dismay-

15

ingly boring if the truth were told. Writers live vicariously through their characters, and through what they observe around them in order to be able to create those characters convincingly. They are the onlookers, the ones who stand outside the window where the party is taking place, looking in but aloof from the laughter and the colour and the wine. They notice which girl is just about to make an idiot of herself, which couple left early, which was the man weeping alone amid the empty bottles – and then hurry home to incorporate the best, most useful tit-bits of character into their novels.

3. Make sure you give your characters the right names. Don't rush to bestow just any name on your hero or heroine. Sometimes you may have a picture of a person in your mind, and it is becoming clearer by the minute. You see the girl's face, her hair, the way she walks, you know what her voice sounds like. But her name? That is more difficult. She does not seem to have a name. Nothing you can think of will suit her.

This is not just foolishness or a display of the artistic temperament. If you feel for whatever reason that you have got to give this brain-child a name, and against your better judgement you allow another character to address her as Mary when you know perfectly well that she is not a Mary, you could do both her and your novel a great deal of harm.

There will be a right name for every character, and until you find the right name, it is better to consciously use a 'working title' which you intend to change later or not refer to the character by name. Margaret Mitchell first called the heroine of her novel of the American Civil War, Pansy O'Hara, and it was only one day when she was preparing the manuscript for publication after it had been accepted that she suddenly crossed the name out and scribbled *Scarlett O'Hara*, which had just sprung to her mind and which she knew instinctively was right.

Daphne du Maurier skilfully crafted *Rebecca* so that the name of the narrator, which another character describes as 'very lovely and unusual', is never actually revealed.

Most novelists are aware of the importance of finding the right names for their characters, the names which will somehow set those characters free to live. The exact way in which this happens must remain one of the mysteries of the creative process, but it has been mentioned by many distinguished writers. Even Charlotte Bronte commented, when writing to her publishers just prior to the publication of *Villette*:

> As to the name of my heroine, I can hardly express what subtelty of thought made me decide upon giving her a cold name; but at first I called her 'Lucy Snowe'... which Snowe I afterwards changed to 'Frost'.
>
> Subsequently I rather regretted the change, and wished it Snowe again. If not too late I should like the alteration to be made now throughout the MS. A *cold* name she must have...

You can say a lot about your heroine or hero in the names you decide to give them. Fashions in Christian names can pinpoint a period and reveal your characters' ages, and even the social strata from which they sprang. Be aware of names.

A woman called Lily or Doris or Violet was probably born in the pre-World War II years into the 'working classes'. The same social class in the fifties produced a crop of Marlenes and Marilyns, amongst others. You're safe with something timeless and classic such as Mary or Anne or Elizabeth – John or Charles or Robert for boys; but note how the different shortened forms will again give away period and social class. 'Bobby' is a different sort of man from 'Rob'; 'Charlie' could never be mistaken for 'Chas'; 'Liz' and 'Beth' and 'Liza' are all distinctive.

4. Remember that your characters have been alive for some time before your novel actually starts, and a lot has happened to them which has made them the people they

are. Some writers find it useful to keep a sort of dossier or file on every person mentioned in the book, listing physical characteristics as well as notes on previous history. This will certainly come in useful later, if you have a mental lapse and forget the colour of someone's hair, or exactly when your hero was born. It is surprising how often such lapses can occur, and even editors or readers don't always pick up on them.

In one novel I wrote, the heroine's eyes altered from blue to green in the middle of the story so that she was actually referred to as 'the girl with the green eyes' in the latter half of the book; but there had been a scene earlier where, on her wedding day, her emotions were described at some length as making her blue eyes almost violet. The amazing thing was that by the time I noticed and, blushing with shame, tried to correct the error, at least three different sets of publishers' readers and editors had read the book for different editions and none of them had mentioned this startling inconsistency. In fairness, I think this is the only time I have done such a thing, but one error is one too many for novelists who want to be considered reliable.

So use your dossiers to fill in information about your characters if this helps you to 'see' them and gives you a feeling of getting to know them. And use the data to keep a check as you write your novel and your characters develop, bringing them up-to-date if necessary as you progress. The only word of caution to add is, don't be tempted, as a lot of would-be novelists are, to spend all your time on files and dossiers rather than attack the real hard graft of writing the actual novel itself.

2
PLOT

ONE of the questions a novelist is most commonly asked is: 'How do you think of your plots?' Thinking of plots is wrongly assumed by many, including new writers, to be an ability which a benevolent providence inexplicably bestows on other authors, but never on oneself.

The plot of your novel is not a structure on its own, something complete in itself, though this misconception is another that is fairly common. At one time there were even 'plotting devices' available for would-be writers to buy, with which they could work out plots for stories by shuffling cards with descriptions of certain characters on them, and seeing which incidents like 'A Quarrel', 'Blackmail' or 'Love at First Sight' tumbled out of the pack. Apparently the view was that once you had your plot rigidly worked out, nothing could go wrong.

The human mind enjoys creating order out of seeming chaos, and possibly the task of racking one's brains trying to relate incidents like 'Blackmail' and 'A Meeting' to each other might have given some writers inspiration. But if their plots were created before their characters had begun to take on flesh and blood, those characters would probably have emerged as almost completely lifeless.

Unless you are writing a detective novel or something similar, where every person's movements and actions have to be carefully charted so that complicated clues and 'red herrings' can be introduced on every page, your plot should spring largely from an awareness of your characters. Characters almost never arise from the plot. When you have some idea of your characters, your plot will follow.

Why, for instance, does a particular incident occur in

Chapter Three? The readers will see clearly, if your characters are well portrayed, that it was because Jane was such a bossy person she couldn't keep her nose out of the affairs of others. From her bossiness and tendency to interfere and 'lay down the law' will spring quite naturally your scene where Paula loses her temper and drives off in a rage, forgetting she had promised to give Jane a lift home. And because Jane, left stranded, either accepts a lift with somebody else or decides to walk, a new relationship can develop – or danger, love, death: whatever your story is going to reveal to us.

Don't wail helplessly that you 'just can't think of a plot' and remain convinced that if only you could get hold of a good one, your novel would somehow write itself. Think of your characters: their ambitions, their desires, their strengths, their weaknesses. Consider how these people will react to each other if you bring them together. Few human beings show absolutely no emotion or feeling as they pass through the events of a day, and your characters are, as we have already mentioned, very solidly based on the qualities of real people.

The fact that your characters will have their good and bad spells, their up and down moods, will provide you with 'reasons why', plausible explanations for new twists and turns in a plot. You cannot be a dictator who imposes the framework of a plot onto the helpless characters in your power. There have to be reasons why things happen as they do – reasons which the readers will accept.

Why did John decide not to mention the fact that he'd had a parking ticket when he got home? Make it obvious to both him and the reader, from his wife's response on his arrival, that she wouldn't have accepted the news in a rational manner. Why did Jenny go out on Tuesday night, when she normally spent the evening at home? If the reader has a vivid picture of Jenny's husband all set to drown his sorrows after a hard day, sprawled in front of the TV surrounded by cans of beer and yelling abuse at the figures on the screen, it won't seem surprising that Jenny suddenly decided she needed some fresh air and a bit of peace and quiet.

The better you come to know your characters, the more you are able to consider what action *they* would take in certain circumstances – rather than biting your nails as you try to imagine what you'd have done yourself or what would 'make a good plot' thereby forcing them into situations which might not suit their personalities – the smoother your plotting will seem to your readers. The best plots are those which don't intrude, so that the reader isn't even aware there's a plot at all.

In some books, readers will tell you, absolutely nothing seems to happen yet they just can't put the book down. This 'un-put-down-able' quality is what most writers would give their whole shelf of reference works for, and it is often the result, in part, of having the confidence to let your characters lead you into the story's developing situations, rather than being bound by a rigid and clumsy 'plotted' framework.*

I have even known a case where an author did in fact start off with a 'plotted' plot, severely structured, into which he pushed any old characters that seemed to suit it. Eventually (he knew from experience) somebody would emerge who refused to conform, wouldn't do what the plot required, took off in another direction and became the central character in the *real* novel that had been in preparation. The 'plotted' plot, having served its purpose in helping the author to find a worthwhile character round which to build his serious work, was discarded, and the new plot was built round the characters as they began to live.

Although it sounds as if I'm advocating a somewhat sloppy approach and hinting that the author just lets the characters do whatever comes into his head with no planning or control, this is not the case. A novel does have to be constructed consciously, decisions have to be made, and it is very important that the shape of the story is clear – and remains clear – in the mind of the writer.

* See also How To Be Un-Put-Down-Able Chapter 18

We will be examining in more detail later how a novel is given its structural form, how it must keep to the theme that should run through it, how climaxes are arranged so that they come at the right moment, and all the other techniques an author uses to build and strengthen a plot. Such structural work can only follow, however, in the wake of what your subconscious hands out to you. Characters who seem to live, and who point the way to exciting turns of the storyline that you'd never have thought up consciously in isolation – these are the 'inspirations' in your story. The hard slogging, the conscious effort, the worry and the struggle to smooth everything out and make it work: this is where technique and craftsmanship builds a realistic foundation for the towering turrets and dizzy pinnacles where your novel reaches into the clouds.

The novelist should have an awareness of his characters, who they are and how they will behave under any given circumstances, and also a clear picture of the various threads of his story and how they are progressing. Somehow, these have to be balanced so that the result seems effortless, believable and gripping to the reader.

HINTS TO HELP YOU CREATE PLOTS

1. Whereas a short story involves only one main conflict between the central character and either someone or something else or some force within himself, with no room for sub-plots, there should be more than one storyline in a novel. You can make a novel richer by careful inclusion of sub-plots, secondary characters and diversions. Often these can underline or emphasise by contrast what is going on in the main story.

A novel should have one theme, however, one 'message' or preoccupation, which runs through it from the beginning to the end. This will overshadow your main story or complement it in some way, and you should never lose sight of it as you progress through the book, nor suddenly alter it and substitute another theme.

Keep at the back of your mind throughout, the final

climax which will take place at the end of the book, even if you are not quite sure how this is to be accomplished or exactly what will happen. Everything should play a part in carrying the reader towards this end, rather than appearing to go off at a tangent. A reader who gets the feeling that he's somehow left the story and wandered into another book might well lose interest and stop reading.

2. You can have large numbers of characters in a novel, but don't bring in people who play no part in the story, or include incidents which are not really relevant. Even though a novel seems to offer a great deal of space, remember the writer's maxim that every word should count. This applies just as much in a novel as in a short story or an article. You cannot afford to be sloppy or care-less or use your novel to indulge your own private little fantasies if you want it to stand up to serious scrutiny. Discipline yourself so that you write tightly and don't waste words – or, if you do this in your first draft, make sure you go through the manuscript with a relentless blue pencil afterwards before you write the final version

3. Remember not to introduce too many characters all at once, or the reader may have difficulty in recalling their names and who they are, in the same way a real person would do if suddenly introduced to a crowd of complete strangers. You know your characters, but be aware that to your reader they are new faces, and allow time for the reader to make each person's acquaintance.

4. Don't include apparently significant incidents or happenings – or anything that hints at further action – unless you intend to pick up these points further on in the narrative. The readers expect everything in a story to have some sort of meaning. If you make a point of letting the hero's sister become blinded in an accident, the readers will be waiting for her blindness and/or the accident to play a vital role in the story.

If two of your characters have a fight and one threatens

to kill the other (unless he's the blustering type who habitually does this and the readers know better than to take any notice), you cannot just forget about this threat. The readers won't. Never introduce anything into a story which does not have some point, some meaning or significance. Every incident in your plot – like every word in the narrative – should be there for a purpose, and if questioned, you should be able to explain what the purpose is, however vaguely.

5. Don't think that if you employ a very dramatic background, such as the events of a war, this will give you a framework for your novel with no further work on your part. Even with the background of war or some similar conflict, the characters still have to resolve their own struggles, which spring from their individual personalities, not just from external events.

In novels set against the background of World War II such as *The Cruel Sea* by Nicholas Monsarrat, *HMS Ulysses* by Alistair MacLean or *Tanamera* by Noel Barber, it is the personal triumphs and tragedies we remember most vividly, rather than the 'historical' aspects of the war. A dramatic setting may even appear boring if the characters through whose eyes we view events are colourless, boring people.

3
SCENE

THE place where your novel is set is just as important as
the characters who will act out the story and the events
which will take place. No reader can identify with creatures who inhabit an unfamiliar world that's quite incom-
prehensible. The feeling of recognition is important that
the readers too have walked similar country pathways –
or, if the story is set in a foreign location, that this particular island is exactly where they'd like to go for a holiday
if they could afford it or if they were lucky enough to meet
a handsome millionaire (like Ross, the hero) who just
happened to own an island or two!

In fantasy and stories which are actually set in other
worlds, it is very necessary that the setting is made credible
to the reader. Tolkien's trilogy *The Lord of the Rings* goes
into immense detail so that readers are swept effortlessly
into the cosmology of Middle Earth. Footnotes, historical
details, even dates, will all give apparent authenticity to a
completely imaginary scene, though readers of lighter
novels would find it odd if footnotes were included. It is
quite possible, however, to make your description of a
beautiful country house more realistic by including, alongside mention of the mellow stonework and Elizabethan
windows, the information that the house was originally
claimed to have been designed by Inigo Jones, but in fact it
was built to a plan copied from one of his originals, with
additions by Sir Harry Fairfax, who built it.

Above all, a reader looks for authenticity, a sense that
the novelist knows the world he or she is writing about, so
even if your knowledge of Inigo Jones (or country pathways or interesting characters like the scissors-grinder in
the streets of northern cities) is rather shaky, never allow
this to become obvious in your novel, Of course you will

want to do some background research. It is possible to create a convincing setting with only a little actual detail, so long as what's given is correct, clear and described with complete authority. There are some readers who make it a habit to forage through novels in the hope of discovering mistakes or errors they can triumphantly point out to author and publisher; but the skilful novelist makes as certain as possible that all facts included in descriptions – how old furniture is restored, or how a sale is conducted at Christies – are correct (barring human error, since even novelists are human!) and then keeps discreetly silent about all the other circumstantial details which he can't be quite sure of.

Many would-be novelists worry about how much scene-setting or description they ought to include, and feel there is a right and a wrong method, so that they'll be committing some grave error if they don't write enough. But this idea of a novel as a sort of cake, with certain ingredients –

7 characters

1 plot

1 sub-plot

3/4 litre description of scene (and so on)

– is not only off-putting but utterly wrong.

Whether a book is a rambling story with loving recon-structions of the scent of honeysuckle round the garden gate, or whether it's a spare, laconic affair with hardly any description at all, will depend entirely on the author. Every writer is different. To some, the inclusion of description will come easily, in a flowing style that fits into the story; to others, there will be no need for the colour of the heroine's hair or the view from the hero's flat ever to be mentioned.

Just because you don't seem to be able to think of descriptions, does not mean your novel will be uncon-vincing. And neither need you worry about where the description should fit in, how story and description are 'put' together. Should I have half a page of each in turn, I was once asked, quite seriously.

The main thing about setting and description is that these are the backgrounds to your story, the places where your characters will live out their loves and hates, their triumphs and tragedies. It is necessary for the readers to be aware of them, at the very least, so they know when they meet the heroine, for instance, the relevant information that she lives in a country village and travels to work as the local doctor's receptionist on her old push-bike.

But if the barest outlines are all you give the readers, this is quite enough. You need to know the background and scene yourself, as thoroughly as possible, but not only is it unnecessary but it would be positively disastrous if you were to reveal everything to the readers and insist on telling them all. Quite often a novelist will only use a fragment of the information – even the research – he has at his disposal, but even though the rest of it might not be included, the fact that is was *there* and the novelist knew it will make all the difference to the narrative's inherent authority.

As the scene of your story provides the background for the action, you use it in the most effective way for you, without any thought of whether there's enough description. The background is static, it is a tool to help you build up believable characters with whom the reader can identify, and you should employ it as such. Put in whatever description you think will help the story along, whatever is necessary to make the characters more real and give authenticity to what you are saying.

Ian Fleming created a larger-than-life hero whose lifestyle was outside the experience of most readers when he introduced James Bond to the reading public, but the genuine knowledge of the locations where the books were set, the details of firearms and other items of spy-thrillery he was able to include – even down to the famous Martini, 'shaken, not stirred' – immediately established Bond as almost as familiar to the readers as their own relatives. Yet if the backgrounds, the firearms – even the Martini – had been the setting for a rather meek little man called Sam Hoggins, who investigated claims for travel agencies, the whole set-up of exotic and glamorous mayhem would have been inappropriate.

So don't think of scene and description as some difficult obstacle that you have to get the knack of. The scene you think up, the setting you employ, the way you describe it, all these should spring from your plot and your characters. Use them as you like, putting in as little or as much as you feel you want to. And never try to include more description than you can comfortably write, or desperately stop yourself in mid-sentence, as it were, with a guilty conviction you've written too much about the scene. Stories can always be edited, but if you lose your confidence in what you are doing, they may never be written at all.

HINTS TO HELP YOU WITH SCENE

1. A mistake made by inexperienced novelists is to follow the trend set by classic writers and use the first chapter to 'set the scene'. Even in great classic novels such openings can, to modern readers, prove hard going. In the hands of novelists who haven't yet learned their trade, the effect is usually catastrophic.

No use saying that Thomas Hardy did it, and pointing out the long, lowering introduction to *The Return of the Native*. Thomas Hardy was not writing today, nor getting published today. But in novels – like *The Return of the Native* – where the scene, or some aspect of it such as the inaccessibility of a mountain peak, for instance, assumes the characteristics of one of the protagonists in the story, you can open with a view of the scene as Hardy does, and give it as much attention as you might give any other character. Be careful not to bore your readers, though. In fact, quite a lot of classic styles and methods of writing – which might well have worked for geniuses of the past – are quite wrong for writers *now*.

Avoid an opening description which takes a bird's-eye view of the scene, and then uses a sort of literary zoom lens to close in on the village, the house, the window, where Cressida, or whoever, is brushing her hair. It's a method which is very tempting because you can clear a lot of explanation out of the way and give the readers a picture of the scene, all in one fell swoop. But readers aren't going to hang about while you sort out your construction problems. They want something a little more sophisticated; they want to see some action right from line one. And it is probably true that description as such – the sort of leisurely, slow-progress, all-encompassing description which has been fashionable in the past – no longer has much appeal to readers increasingly accustomed to the quick-fire, half-a-minute impact of media advertising. The days of the naive, well-meaning writer who writes a successful novel by describing activities in her own small village are long past.

2. If you are setting your novel in a world with which readers are not likely to be familiar – for instance, the Arctic or a missile base – make sure you include quite a lot of background detail, both to give credibility and so that readers will begin to feel at ease in the confines of your novel. The more familiar the scene and the surroundings become, the more they will enjoy the story and the sense of familiarity with a different way of life.

3. Bear in mind that the places and scenes in your novel should be described to the readers according to which character is your principal character, if not for the whole book, then at that time in the story. Say that a cathedral plays quite a large part in the novel, and a lot of the activity takes place within its environs. How you describe it will depend on whether your readers are viewing the action through the eyes of the bishop, the local businessman who is trying to open a casino, a young tourist interested in architecture or a girl who's just been told she is dying of cancer. Remember that in fiction, as in real life, the scene looks different to different people. Their interests, preoccupations, awarenesses, as well as personal likes and dislikes, will govern what they see, and it is always more effective if you avoid the omnipotent 'narrator' form

of description and show the scenes as your characters see them.

4. In the same way as the 'setting the scene' opening chapter, and the bird's-eye view zooming in on your principal character, avoid such contrived methods of description as following the course of a river and commenting on the various buildings along the bank; starting Chapter One with the postman or delivery-man, or anyone who will be visiting the whole cast of characters, setting out and either exchanging chat with them or – in the case of the postman – speculating on who has sent their mail, thus introducing the readers to the different strands you will weave into the plot.

5. If you feel you must include extracts from old-fashioned guide-books on the quaint and whimsical scenes of olden days in the area where your novel is set, try to make sure they are 'read' by one of the characters, rather than simply quoted by yourself.

6. You can allow yourself a certain amount of licence with real places, move a street or change the houses round, but acknowledge this if you do it, or readers will think you were careless and lazy over research. Inaccurate novelists are not popular. Don't meddle with any well-known buildings, scenes or places, altering the Royal Pavilion, for instance, or removing the graveyard and church outside the Parsonage at Haworth. If you want to use a real place, take the trouble to do your research so that your descriptions will be correct. Make sure the sun rises and sets in the right direction and rivers flow the right way. Some reader will certainly notice if you describe a beautiful sunset over the castle in Edinburgh, from a position where the sun would have set in the east!

4
DIALOGUE

APART from narrative and description, which are familiar enough to most people as part of their everyday speech, a novel contains dialogue – reported conversations between the characters. The prospect of trying to create effective dialogue can deter even the most cultured and intelligent writers, because reporting conversations *between imaginary people* is not something we normally do.

Writing dialogue is a skill that isn't taught in schools or in literature classes. It can appear to bristle with problems – how do I know whether to keep putting in the 'he saids' and 'she saids' or leave some of them out? Should I try to alter 'saids' to 'expostulated' or 'enquired', so there is less repetition? Will my dialogue sound real? I don't think I'm very aware of how people talk; I've never written fiction before.

A novelist should cultivate an ear for the spoken word. Part of your preparation for attempting a successful novel should be to listen unashamedly to any conversations you might overhear on buses, on trains, in queues, in shops. Everywhere you go, be aware of what the people around you are saying to each other, and how they are saying it. This need not necessarily mean you wander round on investigations with a cassette recorder, studying the speaking patterns of the natives. Your novel may be one of those which contains hardly any dialogue and your style may be such that you know with absolute certainty you'll *never* have any characters in your books who don't come from the same background and social class as yourself. But even so, the variations in how people talk, how they express themselves, how they cover up their real meanings and tell lies in order to reveal the truth, are not just confined to members of different social classes.

The words ordinary people use, and the way they use

31

them, make up the raw material for fictional conversation and dialogue. You will need to have an ever-ready ear for the striking phrase, the topical – or unfashionable – use of slang, the way pauses and half-finished sentences can be employed. Simply listen and be aware of what you hear.

The 'raw material' of everyday conversation cannot, however, be transferred wholesale into the pages of a novel. Even though dialogue has to seem real and the conversations between your characters must appear utterly convincing, all dialogue in fiction is used for effect and is therefore very artificial. Every word has to count, unlike a conversation in real life which can be full of vague generalities and woolliness. This is why characters in novels seem to be such clear and well-defined people (unless the novelist has deliberately aimed for a cluttered effect). Even the half-choked utterances, the broken phrases which seem to be suggesting deep feeling and an inability to express emotion, have been pared down by the novelist to hit home in exactly the right way.

You should think of dialogue as a rather high-spirited horse, which needs to be first understood, known, gentled – yet allowed its dignity – and then guided by you in the ways you want it to go and for your own specific ends. Get to know popular usage of words, listen to speech in ordinary and extraordinary situations, and then use this information selectively and carefully to get the effects you want in your novel.

You may find, as a lot of novelists do, that your characters mysteriously come to life and run away with the things they say, so that it never seems as though *you're* putting words in their mouths at all.

Even more strange is the fact that a novelist does not usually know in advance what people are going to say to each other when they have their long anticipated 'meeting' in Chapter Seven or confrontation at the end. A novelist will wait as eagerly as his readers to see what emerges when two characters begin to talk to each other. Sometimes the result will be as much of a surprise to the novelist as to the readers, and can even disrupt his carefully laid plot or reveal depths he'd never suspected in these apparently quite innocuous people.

This does not mean that some novelists have a gift or talent for being able to write dialogue and others haven't. Even the most intuitive creator of dazzling and brilliant conversations within the pages of his novel would never have been able to write them if he had not been acutely aware of what people say and don't say in real life, and how they express feelings and communicate and block other people's attempts to get through and break their defences.

A very large percentage of novelists work with their subconscious far more than they realise, but even a subconscious can only use the material within it. A dull, unresponsive person who has never taken any notice of anything said around him is highly unlikely to begin to turn out literary gems of wisdom and maturity. So if you keep an open and enquiring mind towards language and speech in common use around you, and think about what you hear, the chances are that much greater that – with or without the assistance of your subconscious – you will write convincing and effective dialogue.

Sometimes, as I have mentioned, dialogue seems to write itself, and it is perfectly possible that a new writer who's never before written fiction will produce good, convincing dialogue with no trouble at all. Maybe the dialogue will not even need to be edited or tightened or touched in any way. On the other hand, if you're finding the conversations in your novel rather hard going and are worried about whether they are good enough, an awareness of what they are made up of – the raw materials – and what they are actually there *for* can help. You can attack the problem in a workman like way and bring some order to the chaos, not feel rather helplessly that 'it's Art' and somehow your inspiration didn't get things quite right.

The purposes of dialogue in a novel are partly to break up the solid text of narrative and make reading easier; partly to give a sense of intimacy and immediacy – of being on the spot when things happen; partly to persuade readers of the reality, humanity and general credibility of the characters. There are innumerable more subtle connotations in dialogue too; but since the main concern of the novelist is that readers should read his novel and find it believable and enthralling, it would merely be wasting time to delve into the intricacies of word suggestion and subliminal use of language to plant ideas. Never become tempted to explore depths of communication in such detail, or you are likely to end up with your novel unwritten and you'll be so cluttered with minutiae that you will never write it.

HINTS TO HELP WITH DIALOGUE

1. There is nothing wrong with repeating 'said' as you detail conversations, and this is preferable to contriving 'exploded' or 'agonised'. The choice of words you use will depend to a certain extent on the type of novel you are writing. In a straight novel, 'said' is probably right, but in comedy it may be effective to use outrageous words like 'exploded'. Be very careful how you employ this sort of style, though.

2. It is not always necessary to include 'he said' or 'she said'. If it suits the book and it is clear which character is speaking, you simply write the speech on its own in inverted commas. If the reader can follow it without losing touch with the participators in the conversation, several pages of speech without a single 'said' are perfectly acceptable*. Remember that the 'he said' and 'she said' are only there to make things easier for the readers, who cannot – as in a play or on a film – see the people who are talking.

With this in mind, use 'he said' or any other comment like: '"No." Joss shook his head slightly' only if you feel it is necessary to keep the scene clear to the readers. A name here and there, a brief mention of some reaction, are all that is necessary for the novelist to keep the scene and the characters clarified for the benefit of those who will read the book.

What matters is the content of each speech, how that

---

*Jane Austen employs this method very elegantly and you can also find it in the work of Alan Plater (for example *The Beiderbecke Tapes*) and Jose Maria Arguedas's *Yawar Fiesta*. (Translated: Frances Horning Barraclough. Published by Quartet Books).

person reacts to another character. The mention of 'said' and the names of those who said it are really a sort of helpful prompting for the reader, but usually play no part in the action.

3. Bear in mind that it is through what your characters say to each other that the depths and complexities of their personalities are revealed. An account of how sensitive and compassionate the heroine is, or what she feels for the hero, will carry far less weight than a few lines where we see her expressing – in however halting a manner – her sensitivity, compassion, or attraction to a man she is not even sure, possibly, that she likes or approves of. People trying to express or repress their feelings, hide what they really think, or conform with the dictates of society while wanting to break everything in sight: dialogue is your medium through which to make all these situations real and compelling in a way that is not possible if you use only narrative.

4. It is the levels on which dialogue is written – the simple speeches that hide conflicting desires or express the exact opposite of what they say – which give richness and depth to your novel. The narrator is expected to tell his readers the truth, whether he is a character in the story or an omnipresent observer. But the characters themselves may struggle throughout the narrative to avoid their own truths, and perhaps will never admit to them. This makes them fallible, and so endears them to the reader, who is all too conscious of his own human weaknesses. Complicated dialogue with large numbers of long words and wonderfully balanced phrases is not half so enthralling as simple half-sentences which, as the reader will know from the working-out of your novel, conceal unutterable depths of feeling.

The content of each speech is what matters in dialogue and even more important is what lies behind that speech – if at this point in the story you want to reveal it – and what your characters do not or *cannot* say.

PART II
CRAFTING YOUR NOVEL

5
MAKING A START

THERE are two viewpoints from which one can look at the beginning of a novel. One is that of the reader, which also encompasses the critical approach and that of an expert in English literature. The other is strictly reserved for people who actually *write* novels and therefore know, as readers, critics and literature professors do not unless they have written one too, what it feels like.

From the reader's point of view, the opening chapter and the first few pages and lines are of immense importance. Would-be novelists have sometimes been advised (by people who know very little about it, I suspect) to keep a notebook of stunning 'opening sentences' to use whenever they are stuck for just the right method of hitting the reader over the head and dragging him into a new novel.

In the past, methods were calculated so that the writer could gain shocking efforts from his opening words. Somebody in the forties or thereabouts propounded the sentence: '"Damn!" said the Duchess' as being so startling and eye-opening that no reader would be able to resist it.

Much has been said about excellent introductions to novels. Sometimes examples are quoted L.P. Hartley's *The Go-Between* opens with the emotive, atmospheric words: 'The past is a foreign country: they do things differently there.' *Anna Karenina*, Tolstoy's tragic study of a woman's passions, begins thoughtfully: 'All happy families are alike but an unhappy family is unhappy after its own fashion.' Charlotte Bronte plunged uncompromisingly into her narrative when she wrote, as the opening to *Jane Eyre* 'There was no possibility of taking a walk that day.'

All of these, and many other openings of novels, are indeed excellent, but they cannot really assist new novelists who are groping for their own best medium of expression, their own opening sentence, which has to be personal to them and (even more important) to the novel. Such calculated methods of finding the most effective, the most startling, the most unforgettable opening lines by weighing up beginnings of other novels might help you to get your brain ticking over and suggest new lines of thought; but they are highly unlikely to bring you the answer you seek if you are worrying about how to start your own novel and waiting for inspiration to strike.

All assessment of the suitability of opening sentences to the theme, the characters and the rest of the novel, is done from the point of view of the reader, the critic, the professor of literature. It is done when the novel has not only been completed, but has also been edited and published. Sometimes, too, it is done with the awareness that the book or the author (or both) is highly regarded in the history of world literature.

The viewpoint from which we, the novelists, look at our openings is very different.

The body of the novel has yet to be written, and we always, however experienced we are, have that niggling worry that something might prevent us from reaching the end. To a novelist, the opening is in the nature of a foothold established so that he can proceed. Sometimes, it is true, novelists polish their work page by page as they go along so that when they reach the end, they don't even have to re-read it, but it is far more likely that you will want to come back to incidents, people or descriptions in the early pages of your novel and alter them in some way, however small, as you progress. Your opening can be hurried, inadequate, or even not there at all because you decided you couldn't get it right and so started off with another character taking his dog for a walk. Do not worry. None of this need affect your novel in the slightest.

A formulated approach to a novel, leaving nothing to imagination – inspiration – the subconscious – would never work except as an interesting novelty, since nothing fresh, no new thoughts or views of life, would ever be added. Suggestions on how to discover an arresting opening for your book, or indeed anything that claims to give you inspiration but is based on lists or averages or 'how the greats did it', might seem to provide you with a walking-stick to get along, a crutch to take your weight; but sooner or later, if you want to be a good novelist, you are going to have to stride out on your own.

Even the lists you make of your own thoughts can be deceptive and might prove more of a hindrance than a help. My own experience is that wonderful 'opening sentences' I have dreamed about never seem to materialise into corresponding plots; the stories and characters I *do* want to write about stubbornly refuse to have anything to do with memorable opening phrases which can be quoted in the *Oxford Dictionary of Quotations*.

It is far better to scribble a few pages of Chapter One, in whatever form, than mess around with lists of 'opening sentences' and analyses of how great novelists grabbed their readers. Get your novel started, if it only consists of three printed-out pages from your word processor and five torn-off sheets from a notepad, covered with crossings out and a splash of coffee.

Take the first step forward, establish your toe-hold. From the first pages you can start that trek to the final scene on page 511; but until you get some part of the novel written, however shakily and in whatever crossed-out and unsatisfactory form, you cannot proceed at all.

For every novelist who starts but gives up before the half-way mark, there are hundreds who are going to write the most superb novel 'when I have the time' or who have even got the time already, but can't seem to settle to Chapter One and never actually write the first word. Don't join their ranks. Write something – write anything – but get going and make a start, or your novel will end up as nothing but a might-have-been.

As with your characters and plot, don't try to cling too close to the early landmarks which guided you along the road into your novel. If the original opening sentence you had in mind doesn't seem to fit when you finally start to write, then let it go and write one that does fit. A novel can bother and worry a new novelist because it never stays still, and it seems to beckon and then disappear so that the whole process of writing is as exhausting as grappling with a ghost in heavy mist. Ideas and thoughts flicker and seem to be gone. When they do reappear the novelist has to be alert to catch them again. So the importance of your opening sentence, paragraph, page and chapter, is that it actually establishes something concrete from which you can work forward into the rest of the novel. You can come back at any time – even at the end – to rewrite or polish your sketchy opening.

When Margaret Mitchell's novel of the Deep South was considered – and accepted enthusiastically – by a reader for Macmillan, it had neither an opening chapter nor a title. (In fact, she said the last chapter was the one she wrote first.) Only when she was settling to the mammoth task of editing her manuscript and working on a finished copy of the text did she evolve the title *Gone with the Wind* and, at some stage, write Chapter One.

Your opening sentence, your opening page, the whole vista which readers see first as they read your book, has to be relevant to what will come later, and an innate part of the whole. Even though you may not have felt very confident in these early pages, and you might not have had much idea about the characters – been feeling your way, as it were – the readers must not be allowed to suspect this. They have to view the scene, as your literary curtain rises, with a conviction that these characters are real, the scene is clear and definite.

This is where a weak or shaky start can prove more useful to you in the long run than a gem of wit or wisdom with which you might have slaved to open your programme. If the beginning seems 'quite good', there is a great temptation to leave it alone; whereas if the beginning is terrible and you know you will have to come back and work on it, you will be able to do your revision at the end with a much greater confidence and knowledge of your plot and your characters.

HINTS TO HELP YOU MAKE A START

1. You're going to write a novel but strangely, whenever you have the opportunity to get down to it, something always seems to crop up which just has to be done instead. Even when you sit down at your desk, the papers need sorting, the reference books are out of order, the pens want refills so you have to slip out to the local shop. All of these are devices well known to writers as means to avoid actually doing any writing at all.

If you want to write a novel, everything in your life might well conspire against you to prove you *have no time*. You have. Everybody has. Some people write at 4.30am. Others settle down at midnight. I wrote a great many of my best novels at a cafe table in a busy city centre, drinking my morning coffee. Another – my first adult novel – was written on bus journeys back and forth to work twelve miles away.

Be hard on yourself. One of the most important skills a writer has to learn is self-discipline. It probably won't be easy, but anyone who told you this was easy money had never written a novel! You'll get your reward in your sense of achievement when you reach the end.

2. Don't be tempted to have long heart-to-hearts with your husband/wife or a close friend, where you explain the plot in detail and recount the whole story. This is one sure way you will lose the novel by 'talking it out'. The spark will fade, the impetus will disappear and you will never write that book at all.

Try to keep it to yourself for as long as possible without telling anybody what you're doing. If you do find you need to confide in somebody, one person from whom you can have some response and on whom you can test your thoughts is enough.

3. Avoid the temptation to keep re-reading and revising your opening pages. Try not to re-read at all, since you are likely to feel utterly discouraged either because what

you've written seems so awful, or because it's so brilliant that you're sure whatever you write next will fall flat. Keep going and don't look back. You can edit, revise, rewrite, even alter completely, once you reach the end.

6
SETTING THE PACE

IN the opening pages, a novelist has to establish the pace of the story – that is, the speed at which events happen. Every novel has its own pace, which will depend on the type of book it is to be. In deep, introspective novels where the characters spend a lot of time thinking about their emotions and indulging in painstaking analysis of themselves and everybody else, the pace has to be quite slow. You couldn't write that sort of intense, condensed prose if you were covering the events of military campaigns in great detail, or a span of twenty years in the life of your heroine.

Slow-paced books will be the thoughtful ones that are filled with reflective comment. Every small detail and incident will count and be meaningful to the characters. A lot of the action will take place within their heads, or in the shifting of relationships. Does this sound like the sort of novel you want to write? Then don't try to set a fast pace and whisk the action forward very quickly. The whole of your novel might cover only a significant weekend, or the events of one summer.

Intensity is the keynote here. Rivalries in a racing-stable leading up to a frantic neck-and-neck race as a climax; car chases across Europe; people leaping off one plane and catching another – this sort of action is physical and is useful as background for novels that are quickly paced, but will disturb the slow pace you want to set.

In this type of novel, it quite often seems as though very little – even nothing – happens, and yet the readers cannot stop reading. Readers of a slow-paced novel have to be drawn into the story much more deeply than those of a fast-paced book. Because slow-paced novels cover smaller areas of experience, but cover them in greater depth, they are inclined to be more haunting than the action-packed books. Francoise Sagan's *Bonjour Tristesse* has this haunting quality and so does the work of Daphne du Maurier. In spite of their strong plots, both *Rebecca* and particularly *My Cousin Rachel* are good examples of slow-pacing and how gripping it can be.

Remember that description in a slow-paced novel takes on considerably more importance than in a fast-moving book. If your characters are inclined to deep analysis and introspection, they will be far more aware of what they see and feel and hear and influenced by it. Whereas a very active character might stride through a wood in autumn, intent on getting to wherever he is going, your characters will find the autumn colours or the rustle of the leaves significant in some manner. For people who exist at such a level of awareness – even though your characters might not live so intensely all the time, only during the important period covered by the book – it is practically impossible to pass through a day without stirring up memories or starting off chains of deep thought.

Novels which start off in a static manner – with a set-piece by the characters – and which don't seem to get off the ground, will not catch the interest of the readers. It is possible that the action will not actually start until page 286, but the readers can still be drawn along in breathless anticipation. In a slow-paced novel, as well as in one where the action starts right away and keeps moving, there has to be the suggestion, the expectation, that something is going to happen. Sheer curiosity should keep your readers glued to the page. But if they decide that obviously nothing worth bothering about will take place – and if they are uninterested in the characters anyway – they will shut the book.

It is worth noting that some readers who start a book will plod determinedly to the last page even if they hate it, in a grim contest of will power with the author. But publishers and publishers' readers have no such scruples about fair play. If they find the book boring and unconvincing – in other words, bad and unpublishable – they will read no further than page two.

I was once asked to comment on the manuscript of a novel by a young woman. Chapter One consisted of an account of various people arriving at a cocktail party. One was described in such a way that he was obviously the hero, but though he was supposedly irresistible and fascinating, he did nothing at all remarkable and said nothing that hinted at interesting action to come.

I mentioned this, adding that so far I found the story boring and the protagonist unconvincing. It was all unnecessary, I pointed out; nothing had happened at the cocktail party, so why couldn't the novel have started later – or earlier – when something *was* happening?

The author explained glibly that she wanted the cocktail party in Chapter One so that, though nothing of any importance took place during the party, she could introduce the characters who were to appear in the story and describe them – and the house which was to be the setting for a lot of the scenes in the novel – without having to bother about descriptions later when the drama was unfolding.

I still maintained that Chapter One was tedious and unnecessary, to which her reply was: 'Yes, but wait until Chapter Four: it gets really interesting once you are into the story.'

I pointed out that neither the publisher nor any potential readers would be likely to wait until Chapter Four: they would expect some action from page one. Nor could she accompany the manuscript herself when it was submitted, to explain to people who read it (as she had explained to me) why she had included a first chapter where nothing happened, and to advise them that things would get more interesting in Chapter Four. However I read on, and after a further off-putting and static interval, I turned to the beginning of one chapter – it might even have been Chapter Four – where the opening lines were: 'I woke with her presence still beside me; her scent on the pillow. But she was gone.'

'That,' I said immediately, 'is the opening of your story. All the rest doesn't matter.'

The details of the cocktail party and background could have been summed up in a few words. The point where the hero found 'she' had gone, and realised he could not exist with her missing from his life – this was where the *pace* started to move and the action got under way.

You will get the point, I am sure. Introductions, explanations, preparing the ground, filling in information so you don't have to do it later – if possible, avoid all these, particularly before you start to indicate that things are happening and let the readers meet the people to whom they are happening.

If you cannot think of a way of getting the story going and you want to move off with a bang, jump right in at the deep end. When I was trying to think of an opening for a historical novel I wanted to write, in which the heroine became involved with a highwayman, I recollected reading the comment many years ago that one of the most dramatic openings ever written was that of Stanley J. Weyman's historical novel *Under the Red Robe*. This, reported the commentator (whose name I have forgotten), opened with the words:

'Marked cards!'

And straight away the readers were at the scene, as the accusation of cheating brought all the card-players to their feet, prepared to defend their honour to the death.

I followed this example by opening my own Chapter One with the phrase:

'Stand and deliver!'

And as the heroine, full of spirited indignation, was forced to descend from her coach at the point of a pistol, the story was in full swing.

7
A PERSONAL VIEW

APART from satisfying the curiosity of readers, a novelist should include more subtle ingredients in his or her book. A long-drawn-out account, which went on and on but didn't seem to get anywhere, might keep the readers turning page after page, but would leave them, once they put the book down, with a hollow sense of disappointment. What did I get from that, they might well ask.

Your book has to have some point to it. There needs to be a reason why it's important people should read this novel. The interwoven threads of events and developments once the action takes off must not be quite so tangled as they appear. You have to be in control of the book and know – well, roughly, anyway – what's going on and what point you want to make.

We have already seen that the book must have an appropriate pace, that it must move and not be static. In your opening pages, you also establish the viewpoint from which the story will be told, and this in turn will affect the events of the plot and how the characters react to them.

If you write in the first person – with one of your characters telling the story as 'I' – this will mean that he or she can only record personal thoughts and feelings. What the other characters think, or what their motives are, will have to be guessed at, since the narrator will never really know.

This state of affairs is one which can provide endless plot development, particularly in romantic fiction, where the device of 'misunderstanding' is used a great deal (even in stories which are told in the third person). In novels involving complicated relationships, one gesture or action can have the stunning impact of a blow. The fact that the narrator may speculate on why so-and-so sent a dozen red roses, and decide in the end that it was intended as an insult, makes the characters human beings, and the story as interesting as gossip about 'those awful people at the end of the street'.

However you choose to tell your story, in the first or the third person, remember that it is the personal viewpoint, the personal element, which makes it gripping and believable to the reader. Your characters will be impossible and odious if they know everything and never make a mistake. If you need to include this sort of character, never let him tell the story himself unless he has some redeeming feature like a sense of humour. Agatha Christie's Hercule Poirot generally knows all the answers, and so does Sherlock Holmes. But consider them for a moment.

In the Sherlock Holmes stories, the narrator is the enthusiastic but bumbling Watson; and Ms Christie took the same formula for the Poirot stories, giving the Belgian detective a 'side-kick' who narrates the stories and occasionally expresses disapproval about the way Poirot is conducting affairs. If the detectives themselves had written their own case-notes, these would have been utterly boring, since their accuracy and ability to guess answers or work them out by logic would have removed much of the most important element in a novel about human beings – uncertainty.

If readers can tell in advance what the end is going to be, and how it will be achieved and why this will happen, the story will obviously not keep them up at nights reading, unable to put the book down. So it is from the personal angles, the weaknesses and blind spots and hang-ups and defences of your characters, which you should begin to convey right from the first page, that you can prepare the ground for believable and enthralling developments to come.

If you decide to write your novel in the first person, it might appear that you have an advantage in the amount of realism and the human qualities you can present from the point of view of the narrator. If the story-teller is a girl of fifteen, for instance, she can narrate in modern slang and pronounce the sort of immediate judgments on people around her that will hit the readers with an impact. Writing in the third person, you might not be able to achieve this rapport with your narrator so easily.

But there are drawbacks to using the first person. You have to remember that though you can benefit from the human limitations of your narrator, you are confined by these limitations when it comes to describing things and events about which the narrator is not supposed to know.

For instance, if the main character walks into a room and is greeted with a chorus of 'Happy Birthday!' and thirty guests waving champagne glasses, flash-bulbs popping as the bemused celebrant registers he has walked into a surprise party, there is no way you could in the same narrative record what happened while the party was being organised, if this were written in the first person and the narrator knew nothing about it until he opened the door.

Events which happen when the narrator is not present, conversations held between other characters – the first person novelist has to miss out on these. But if your novel will be a very long one or will cover a large canvas – various different locales and a huge cast of characters, or many years and several generations for example – it is better to tell the story in the third person, since although this cannot afford the same level of intimacy with the narrator, it offers more opportunity to cope with the demands of your story.

8
THEME – AND VARIATIONS

So the pace of your novel and the viewpoint you use to tell the story are going to assist you to grip your readers and carry them forward with you – and with your characters – to the very last page. But the question of why readers should read this particular work, rather than a racing paper or even something far more useful about psychology or how to make money from keeping sheep and weaving the wool, also has to be broached satisfactorily at an early stage in the proceedings. It need not be answered in the minds of your readers just yet – the novel's final comment should come near the end, if not in the closing sentences on the last page. But you must be aware yourself of what sort of satisfaction, what emotional food, what comfort for the soul, you are offering your readers.

A story with no point to it, which just goes on and on, will leave readers disappointed. We've seen that they are likely to enquire about the purpose of the book and decide it isn't worth wasting time on.

Of course, everyone knows a novel has to have a plot. The plot will explain how everything happened and somehow link the incidents in the story together. Isn't that enough?

No, it isn't. You need a plot which gives the story a shape, but you also need some sort of richness, depth, some extra quality which leaves readers feeling glad they read this novel. You want them to feel they have received more than just the bare bones of a story from your pages, more than just an insight into amusing and believable characters, more than just an interesting 'read'. All good novels possess this extra-special quality to some degree, and it comes from various intangible ingredients – the novelist's own personality, view of life and ability to comment on the world and empathise with the human condition. Mainly, though, we can sum it up at this stage in one word – theme.

Every novel has a theme, however slender, however unobtrusive. A novel has to say *something* to the reader, put forward some point which the narrative illustrates and proves. While not preaching a sermon, the novel has to make itself heard. The way it does this – the fact that it has a deeper message than might appear on the surface – gives it richness and depth and quality.

In most popular novels the themes are quite simple. Crime stories, for instance, have themes which can be roughly summed up as 'Crime will not pay'. Romances vary their themes from 'Love will find a way' to 'Home is where the heart is' to 'Love is more precious than gold'. Large-scale blockbusters about people who rise from obscure backgrounds to carve out empires for themselves usually work on some form of 'Was it all worth it?'; in other words, the underlying theme is really 'Quality is better than quantity' or 'Ambition destroys while bestowing'.

Exploring the themes of novels can be a fascinating business, although again, if the writer is not careful, it can become a pleasurable substitute for actually sitting down and getting on with writing your own masterpiece. And don't let the fact that many books are of the 'formula' variety put you off.

Because romantic novels, for example, always contain the same basic messages this gives the reader a sense of security, a feeling of 'rightness'. She or he would be dismayed if she read a 'romantic' novel where the theme was 'Men are beasts, but keep them chained and on a tight leash, and they're just about bearable'.

Are you getting the message yourself now? What does your own novel tell the reader? What does it say after the last page has been read and the cover closed? Will it be thin and superficial and leave the reader feeling sorry he bothered to plough on to the end, since he couldn't care less about the fact that Ethel has gone and Tom has decided to be a monk?

You may be feeling rather proud of yourself because you have had the theme of your novel in mind right from the start, when you first dreamed up the idea for the plot. But let us examine some more themes. There are a few nasty pitfalls into which I would hate you to fall.

Themes which are utterly negative, like 'War is totally destructive' (in which every character is wiped out and not a bird stirs over the desolate landscape at the end) or 'No human being can be trusted' (in which the protagonist is blackmailed, mugged, seduced, robbed, betrayed, and so on, by everybody he knows, including his dear old Granny) are not likely to produce good novels. They work if they are written as humour or black humour, but a humorous account of war will probably have a completely different theme from a straightforward, serious story.

The reason why utterly negative themes don't work is that because readers identify with the characters in the books they read, and because they themselves are constantly seeking reassurance that there is some sort of order, some sense of rightness and fitness, some *sense* in the chaos of living, they will find such a book gives them nothing good, or positive to remember and take with them after they have read it.

Gratuitous brutality, sadism, pessimism and other such self-indulgences which warped, sick or perverted minds require for their own satisfaction should not be inflicted on helpless readers in the guise of novels.

What readers look for – quite unconsciously – in any novel is some sense of justification, a satisfactory feeling that however difficult life appears, the characters who are waiting on page one will somehow, by the time the story is over, set an example, show how things can (or ought to) be done – and if the story ends sadly, prove that the struggling, the sacrifice, the heroism, was not in vain. Most novels, if they are not pure escapism, deal with some sort of struggle, either in relationships or to achieve maturity or wisdom, to accept what cannot be changed, to over-come impossible odds.

It is not surprising that novelists should be preoccupied with struggle, journeying, progression, growth, since this, after all, is what all life is about. Though artificial in almost every way, a good novel keeps as close to reality as possible.

Try to give your novel an up-beat theme. As I have said, this need not be 'preachy' or obvious, but the best novels are those which give something to the world that it is glad to take and keep. Was Dickens mushy? Was *Vanity Fair* sentimental? Are *Jane Eyre* and *The Tenant of Wildfell Hall* old-fashioned and unreadable because they ring with passionate conviction that one should cling to virtue and not fall prey to temptation?

In the desolate landscape, let some small bird sing, some hand reach out to the groping hand beside it. Always try to leave your readers, however harrowing your novel may be, with hope.

9
IN THE MOOD

O NCE a novel is actually under way, it is very difficult
suddenly to alter the mood from comic to tragic, say,
or from teeth-clenching melodrama to witty under playing
of the situation. So it is as well to be aware as soon as
possible of the sort of mood you want to pervade your
novel, and to establish it as early on as you can.

The mood of a novel is sometimes obvious right from
the first word. It would be impossible, for instance, to
suppose after reading the opening lines of H.E. Bates's
exuberant *The Darling Buds of May*, that we were in for a
tear-jerking experience. Life and light and laughter lift us
on every side as we begin:

> After distributing the eight ice-creams – they were the
> largest vanilla, chocolate and raspberry super-
> bumpers, each in yellow, brown and almost purple
> stripes – Pop Larkin climbed up into the cab of the
> gentian blue, home-painted thirty-hundredweight
> truck, laughing happily.
>
> 'Perfick wevver! You kids all right at the back
> there? Ma, hitch up a bit!'
>
> Ma, in her salmon jumper, was almost two yards
> wide.
>
> 'I said you kids all right there?'
>
> 'How do you think they can hear,' Ma said, 'with
> you revving up all the time?'
>
> Pop laughed again and let the engine idle. The
> strong May sunlight, the first hot sun of the year,
> made the bonnet of the truck gleam like brilliant blue
> enamel. All down the road, winding through the
> valley, miles of pink apple orchards were in late
> bloom, showing petals like light confetti.

Contrast the mood of that opening with this, which also features the beauty of nature, but in an entirely different way:

I can't see the sun right now; there's an angel in the way.

As I lie here in the short-cropped grass with my eyes just half open a butterfly alights on the carved angel's head. It stays only a few seconds – its wings opening and closing – then takes off, fluttering away, dancing up and down over the grey stone wall.

Everything around me makes a picture of the greatest calm and serenity. And so it should. This spot, I tell myself, should be peaceful by definition. Yet often I wonder about that...

Bernard Taylor's eerie suspense/horror chiller *Sweetheart Sweetheart* grips the reader in these opening lines with the slightly melancholy, out-of-focus feeling that reality is not quite what it seems, things are not as they appear. Readers would be shocked if, ten pages later, this disembodied, brooding mood was shattered and they were treated to some pantomime humour. They would feel cheated if the end of the novel turned into a merry romp with a traditional 'wedding bells' ending.

One of the most useful and valuable skills you can culti-vate as a novelist is a sense of mood. Mood has nothing to do with the plot for your novel, the story, the pace or the theme. There can be funny novels about murder or death, tragic and serious novels about devoted love, horrific novels about childish games. Many apparently witty books are in fact making a serious comment on their theme; serious novels may well be pointing to the comedy of the situations they describe.

Some novels don't seem to have a mood, and this need not be a drawback, so don't worry if your novel is one of these. When, on considering material for this chapter, I looked through my own published novels, I was amazed to discover that I could find only two which seemed satisfactory in that they established mood right at the beginning. Even more staggering was the discovery that my wittiest novel did not have the slightest indication on the first page that it was amusing at all.

So immediately establishing mood is not the most important thing; what *is* important is that the mood should remain constant throughout – or, if it is changed, that the change should be done skilfully, and this is usually something a new novelist is not equipped to handle. Try to be aware of the mood – however vaguely – of your novel, and once it is set, don't suddenly change it.

It can help to think about mood as the type of music which would be on the soundtrack when you sold the film rights and Hollywood produced the 'film of the book'. What sort of music can you imagine in the background of your novel? Something light, syncopated, witty? Sweeping and epic? Romantic? Modern and electronic?

How you envisage the 'mood music' does not really matter, so long as the style doesn't suddenly stop being Glenn Miller and turn into Bartok. Strangely, people who would recognise inconsistencies of this sort in other forms of art can be blind to it in writing.

I read a novel by a highly cultured and erudite woman, who was genuinely puzzled because her manuscript kept being rejected by publishers. Why, she asked? When I had read it, I was able to explain that she had, in effect, got her soundtrack muddled up and the moods confused. She had written a novel in a romantic mood, where the heroine was starry-eyed and orange blossoms and wedding bells provided the happy ending, but into this was incorporated a subplot involving the heroine's incestuous relationship with her father. It was brutal and stark, and the mood should have been created to suit it. Instead, both moods, the romantic and the stark, ran alongside each other and were utterly incompatible. The reason why the book didn't work, I tried to explain to her, was because she had put together what were in effect two different novels, and hoped they would fit. Two 'soundtracks' were playing at the same time as one read her book, each cancelled the other out.

So be sure you are quite clear, as your book unfolds, of the mood in which you want your readers to read. It need not be the same as your own mood as you write. Hilarious novels have been written by novelists who were in the depths of depression – and even if you are having a mad fling where everything in the world is glorious, don't try to infuse this vivacity into your novel if you have established an intense, rather sombre mood, or a chilling atmosphere of suspenseful horror. The good novelist has to learn to switch his own mood and emotions on and off when he settles down to write another chapter or two, not let it spill over onto the page.

Like an actor who can paint on a happy or a tragic face, a novelist has to keep himself in the background when it's time for his characters to take the stage.

INTERLUDE
THE STORY SO FAR

A novelist hard at work on his novel has no idea when he passes from the 'beginning' to the 'middle', or from the central 'middle section' to the build-up for the 'end'. That is, unless every detail of the book, every small incident, development of the plot, sentence spoken by the characters, has been meticulously planned in advance and the actual writing of the narrative is merely a matter of filling in the spaces between the planning.

Generally, a novelist is too close to his novel to see the shape and framework clearly. His subconscious does this for him and prompts him if he seems to be heading in the wrong direction. Mostly, he simply plods on in the optimistic hope that somehow or another, inspiration will enable him to fill up enough pages before the story has run itself into the ground or that final, unforgettable paragraph he's had in mind from the start can't be put off any longer.

Each part – each section – of your novel will, however, require skills and techniques that enable you to cope specifically with the beginning, say, or the development in the middle section, or the end. We have so far examined the problems you should be aware of before you begin to write and when you make a start on the opening chapters. We've dealt with what we can assume will eventually (when your book is being studied in school and colleges!) be described as your approach to the novel, and how you introduce the story to the readers, and the readers to the story.

The beginning of any novel – how long the introductory

scenes should be for instance, before the readers are allowed to sniff the real meat of the plot – is impossible to determine. Readers need a little time – a few pages at least – to feel the characters are familiar and that they know who Agathe and Mouche are when these ladies wander in from the streets of Paris, or what connection Father O'Malley has with the hero's stepmother in County Down; or which one of the Presidentes whose armies are hurling bombs at each other is actually the real Presidente of this tin-pot regime , for goodness' sake!

You can feel you have passed the signpost that says 'beginning' when your plot is finding its feet, the story seems to be taking off and is becoming more absorbing by the minute, and the characters are more real to you than your husband/wife, children or grand-children. There is a good, solid feeling to a novel that is progressing well. You'll have moments of agonising doubt and uncertainty as you go on – and after all, a good beginning doesn't mean a thing; it's a long way to the end, *if* we ever reach it – you'll be tempted to abandon the whole idea, your novel will drive you crazy. But nothing can beat the sensation of knowing your book is alive, it's taking shape under your pen or typewriter keys, and it's working with everything coming together and falling into place.

Once you've passed the jumping-off point of actually starting your novel and are into the real hard graft, when you are actually wrestling with the problems of construction and development, *then* you are probably heading for the central section – which is much the longest part – of your book.

Everything in a novel, the plot, the characters, the theme, the pace and mood, should be woven together so that the effect on a reader is that of something complete. In a wonderfully executed tapestry, the observer does not examine the blue threads, then the red ones; in a novel, there is similarly something wrong if readers feel they can split the story into all its component parts, and knowledgeably discuss the elevated style and theme as opposed to the rather provincial nature of the characterisation and positively adolescent dialogue.

Certainly it is possible to do this with a novel – people have been pulling books apart for years, imagining they will find the secret of literary skill at the centre, like the kernel of a nut. But the success or failure of your novel will rest on the immediate impact it has on your readers as they read it, both for the first time and later. A good novel is an experience, not just a story, and that experience has to be total, something complete which the readers feel and live, not a theoretical exercise on who can put the best bits and pieces together in the cleverest manner.

The novelist's task is therefore not only to write a good novel but to ensure that the readers are unaware of the machinery behind the scenes, the tangled threads on the reverse of that glorious tapestry, as it were. All great art appears effortless. 'But that's so easy', people cry. 'I could do it myself, standing on my head!'

The artist – whether writer, composer, sculptor or painter – will smile a little at such reactions from readers, audience, observers, and say nothing. He alone knows about the long sleepless nights, the torments of struggling with plots or themes or interpretations that wouldn't work out, the crossings-out or torn-up manuscript paper, the times when he decided to give the whole thing up because it was quite obvious that he was utterly incapable of producing anything and he'd just been kidding himself he had any talent at all.

If any of your readers can detect the hard work and effort, all the trouble you went to as you wrote your novel, then that effort will have been largely wasted. The really skilful writer is one whose readers are convinced they could do as well, if not better, if they only had the time to sit down and throw something together on a note-pad.

But the first step to a successful novel is to get the basic construction completed. All the polishing and editing comes later. As a convenient guide for reference, a check list follows, recapping on the main points that have been made to help you with the opening of your novel and the early chapters.

INTERLUDE
CHECK LIST

1. Be careful not to write your novel as some form of therapy, or because of strong convictions which would be more suited to a non-fiction format, if you want to get it considered seriously by publishers.

2. Be conscious that you are writing for today's readers. Even if setting your novel in the historical past or your own younger days, make sure you are presenting that period in a way which will interest and attract people *now*.

3. Do not use styles, colloquialisms, speech or thinking patterns of earlier eras unless you are doing this consciously and deliberately for some reason – as, for instance, in a parody.

4. Be aware of the sex, age and social background of your probable readers. Once you think you know whom you are writing for and aiming your book at, try not to include effects or changes of attitude and viewpoint aimed at other audiences, which will upset the balance.

5. Don't try to include everything you have to say in your first novel. Put in only what is relevant and keep other ideas for future books.

6. Don't try to write about things you personally cannot comprehend or do not believe in, unless you are making some sort of interesting point of conflict among the characters as part of the story. Don't go against your own sense

of decency or integrity. It never works; the sham and falsity is instantly visible to an expert eye (like that of a publisher).

7. Follow the hints in Part One, Chapter One to help you create your characters.

8. Train yourself to be aware of things and people around you in day-to-day living. Watch and listen. Other people are your raw material. Learn how to use them – or parts of them, bits and pieces of them – in your writing so that what you write is authentic.

9. Be certain your characters have the names that are right for them. Take trouble over this until you are happy with the result.

10. Be aware of your characters as people with past histories, who have lived full lives before your novel actually starts. Keep records or dossiers on their previous years, updated as the novel progresses, if it helps you to have relevant facts easily available. But don't let the compiling of records become an end in itself.

11. Decide carefully which is better for your story, a first person or third person narrator. Be aware of the advantages and limitations of each.

12. Be aware of conversation around you, wherever you are, so that you can create believable dialogue by using what you hear selectively.

13. Use dialogue to express character and to give richness and depth to your book. When reporting what characters say, have all the unspoken things they do not say in mind as well.

14. Bear your characters in mind when you are considering your plot. The plot will arise from what sort of

people your characters are. How they behave will affect what is likely to happen further on in the development of the book.

15. Make sure your plot is suited to the characters who act it out and that if necessary you can alter events as your characters seem to dictate, rather than insisting on a 'planned' plot which rules out spontaneity.

16. Do not ignore the promptings of your subconscious, even if this means altering the whole story. Let your subconscious work for you.

17. Keep the theme of your story clear in your mind. A novel should have only one theme or preoccupation, but your main storyline should be bolstered by sub-plots, secondary plots and the activities of supporting characters.

18. Be clear about what your novel is saying to readers – the theme. Make sure that what it is saying is *worth* saying and not something utterly down-beat and negative. Readers know life is awful, they know all about suffering and grief and how difficult it is to cope. They don't want a gloomily nodding head and a 'Yes, it's shocking, this thing they call life, I couldn't agree more.' What they want is for an author to take them away from all that, or else to lift them above it, or to reveal unexpectedly blooming beauty where that desolate war-torn landscape was barren and bare. If you have nothing to say to your readers about life except how awful it is, then don't write a novel, write to *The Times* and complain about the state of the country or the government.

19. Orchestrate your novel in your own mind as you progress with 'mood-music' which will suit it. And though you must vary the shades of that mood, and may even cover subjects and topics which might not appear to fit into the mood, do not jump about from one mood to another so that the work you are writing changes from

stark realism to romance to witty throwaway and back again. Keep the overall outlook of your book consistent and this will give it unity.

20. Remember that everything in a novel – characters, incidents, scenes – should be there for a purpose. Don't waste your own time and the reader's with rambling irrelevancies.

21. Be certain your setting is authentic but unobstrusive. Include as much or as little description as you feel suits your book.

22. Give your readers variety through the shifting views of different characters and the way scenes look to them individually.

23. Don't worry about a stunning opening sentence for your novel. Just get started with something that will give you a foundation on which to work.

24. Organise your days (and nights) to allow yourself time to write and don't let yourself be distracted from serious work by trifling minutiae.

25. Try to avoid any inaccuracy. Check details if you mention them, and acknowledge any 'novelist's license' you may have taken.

26. Don't start acting the part of 'the Great Author' and holding forth at length to anyone who will listen about your wonderful opus. (Not until you've actually written the book, at least. Even then, avoid a lot of pomp and circumstance when you talk about your work.) Ideas can be talked out, freshness and spontaneity lost because you discussed developments at such great length that you wanted to forget them afterwards, not write them up.

27. Remember that nothing is a substitute for actually

sitting down and getting your book written. There are no short cuts.

28. Be aware of the pace you need to set in your novel, whether slow and intense, or quicker with more physical activity. Incorporate pace into the rough planning of your plot as you see it at this stage, and keep the speed at which the story will unfold suited to the type of book you are writing.

29. Make sure the novel is not static. Drop hints, make promises of further interesting action and complication so that the reader is intrigued and is drawn by curiosity and anticipation to read on.

INTERLUDE
TITLE SEQUENCE

OH, so you finally got round to thinking about the title? About time too, if you ask me. What's the point of handing out assistance with a title when I'm half-way through my novel? Surely the title should be the first thing a novelist is concerned with; even before he starts writing he wants to know what the book is called, doesn't he?

Well, you might imagine so, but in fact the people who worry themselves to death about their titles are the sort of writers we can charitably describe as enthusiastic amateurs. Professional novelists are accustomed to tackling their books with nothing more than a 'working title' to go on: in my own case, this is usually the name of my heroine, so that I refer to the half-written book as *Sophy* or *Emily* or *Jenni*. In all three of those cases, the title stayed the same after I had finished the novel, simply because I couldn't think of anything better to call the story.

'Thinking up a *good* title' is yet another of those misleading and time-wasting occupations which can prevent the less strong-willed writer from actually completing serious work. You can waste months – even years – grubbing in books of quotations and poetry looking for that 'just right' phrase or those apt few words to sum up your great epic, and its theme and subject and scope and view of humanity. In most cases you are quite likely to be told that the title is not 'commercial' and asked by your publishers to change it. So think of all that wasted effort!

The title, in fact, is the least important aspect of your novel to worry about. Titles really do not matter as much as people think. For one thing, fashions in the titles of books change in the same way that make-up and hair styles change every year. As I write, the trend is for novels with simple titles, some of one word only like Jilly Cooper's *Rivals* or *Riders*. If you wrote a stunning block-buster about the world of photographic modelling and wanted to emphasise that the models were so much 'meat' to your gang of high-powered villains, you might think of calling your book *The Flesh is Weak*, but a publisher would probably prefer something stark like the word *Flesh* on its own. If you had gone even further and unearthed some obscure quotation from one of the lesser Elizabethan poets, the chances are that it would almost certainly be swept to one side immediately. The best thing to do with a title is to offer your own but be prepared to alter it if requested to do so.

From my own experience, I can report that *all* the books I wrote which (so I considered) had particularly impressive titles – two of them being *The Candles of Night* and *The Lure of the Falcon* – came unstuck. *The Candles of Night*. I scrapped after much rejection, then rewrote because I thought the plot had possibilities, and it eventually appeared as *Sing No Sad Songs*. I can't really say the new title has enhanced it – I only used that because the story concerned music and a girl with a glorious voice. *The Lure of the Falcon* was similarly rejected and after some rewriting appeared as *Castle of Love* – which is very vague and says almost nothing about the story.

The real moral here, though, lies in what I feel to have been one of the most traumatic incidents in my personal writing career. I actually thought up a brilliant title on one occasion, and 'sold' the idea to a publisher on the strength of that title and a vague outline alone. Plans were being made to promote the book; coloured brochures were even being talked about. But when the crunch came, I found that I was unable to write the novel. I struggled with it for several months and had to admit defeat. In the end I used the experience of trying to write this particular novel in another book, so it wasn't wasted – nothing ever is in writing. But brilliant title and all came to nothing.

Novelists do sometimes sell their new books on a title and an outline, but remember that it's a long way from presenting your title to handing in the completed manuscript. Take my experience as a cautionary tale.

Most titles now famous, those which are household words, only sound so impressive because their writers are recognised as great. Take Dickens, for instance. Many of his novels are called – as I have mentioned with 'working titles' – by the name of the central character: *Nicholas Nickleby, Oliver Twist*. Other well-known novels also use just the name of a person in the story: *Catriona*, Hugh Walpole's *Judith Paris* and *Vanessa, Agnes Grey, Silas Marner, Clarissa Harlowe, Pamela*. This practice is in fact more common than you might imagine, and needs absolutely no skill or poetic discrimination on the part of the novelist once the names of the characters have been satisfactorily settled.

Most other famous titles are just as straightforward if you examine them. *Bleak House* and *A Tale of Two Cities*, which now glitter with literary glamour, are actually quite plain as titles go, and would not inspire a modern reader to pick up the book on a station bookstall, unless it had 'classic novel' or 'The Book of the Film' splashed across it.

A lot of the mystique of titles comes from what happens to a book after it is published. If you wrote the great new classic of the century and called it *2133* or *Theseus* you might well achieve the same acclaim the literary world now gives to the writers of *1984* and *Ulysses*, but your title on a bundle of manuscript would be highly unlikely to raise the temperature in a publisher's office.

Remember again that the writer is in a unique position when it comes to writing a novel. The rest of the world does not know your characters, nor the plot you have in mind to describe to them. Your book is a completely unknown quantity, your title – whatever it is – is strange and does not ring bells in their minds. The fact that you have spent hours thinking up your title, months writing the book, means nothing to potential readers. They didn't ask you to do it, and they do not owe you anything because you've slaved so hard to produce this work for their enjoyment.

Simply, you have to sell the book to them, and if a publisher is willing to publish it and suggests that *Concrete* is a better title that your own sensitive, much-thought-over quote from Sir Thomas Wyatt, we owe him our support. In years to come, when *Concrete* has been recognised as the work of fire and passion it undoubtedly is, people at station bookstalls will feel the same thrill when they look at a *Concrete* cover that people in the thirties felt as they picked up a copy of Cronin's *The Citadel*, James Hilton's *Goodbye Mr Chips* or Priestley's *The Good Companions*. Your title, then, only needs to be a working one throughout, something to refer to the book by for convenience. If you do happen to be struck with inspiration and think of some irresistible phrase which is so suitable it just has to be right, this is all to the good, but don't think something has gone wrong if your mind remains a complete blank and you can't think of anything at all that sounds like a title. Your publisher may suggest something, but if nobody can think of any good, snappy, eyecatching title and you settle for what seems a rather feeble second-rate effort, don't worry. It is surprising what success can do to even a second-rate apology for a title. One of my novels was originally titled *The House in Gloucester Place* but this had to be ruled right out because, unknown to me, there was a notorious house in the real Gloucester Place in London which had nothing to do with the story but which readers might have found misleading.

I could not think of anything else as a title, nor could anyone in the publisher's office. We played around with several suggestions and eventually, in desperation titled the book *Leo Possessed*. It sold into paperback and to the USA and for me that title will always gleam now with a very special lustre.

One useful point to remember is that the title of a *successful* novel – whatever it might be – always sounds better than the most thought-provoking, erudite, poetic, sensitive title on any pile of manuscript. And you as a successful author will find that *Concrete*, when you are referring to it in interviews as your newly published book, will ring more golden and gleam brighter every time you say it and every time you look at the cover.

Whatever your book ends up being called, you are likely to have the same growing conviction in every case, once the novel has actually come into existence in published form.*

---

* Further information about titles in Part IV, THE GENRE NOVEL.

10
WISH ME LUCK
OR HOW TO BE ABLE TO KEEP ON WRITING

MOST novelists are to some extent superstitious about their work. You may find, as you progress into the central section of your book, that you begin to get superstitious quirks yourself. You may feel, for instance, that you write better at a certain time of day – early in the morning or after everyone else has gone to bed. You may become convinced that you need your typewriter or word processor at a certain angle, your desk in a certain part of the room; you may find you write your early drafts of the book best on torn-off scrap paper rather than the handsome pad bound in royal blue that you intended to keep your rough copy in to present later – corrections and all – to the British Museum.

Do not allow yourself to be talked out of such fanciful notions if they occur. Humour these whims so long as they are reasonable and not just more cunning excuses to avoid actually getting down to work. Follow any procedure, such as providing whatever you feel you need within reach of your hand even if you never use it, having music playing if this gives you inspiration or allowing for cups of chicken soup or herb tea if you feel you have to keep yourself going with this particular nourishment.

Don't be ashamed, either, if you want to have some sort of good-luck talisman or token near you as you write. For years, I wrote with the same Parker fountain pen, and was unable to write at all if it ran out of ink. I called it – quite seriously – my 'lucky pen' and never went anywhere without it, regarding it as one of my most essential posses-sions. I quite literally could not work with any other pen.

All this is not as ridiculous as it might seem. The main problem, once you have passed the 'beginning' of your novel, is simply to keep going. Human nature being what it is, the novelist can progress better with milestones of some sort or familiar rituals which will give him confidence as he settles down for another stint.

The way you organise your time and resources and prepare yourself to tackle the sixty, seventy or eighty thou-sand words you have set yourself to write can make all the difference between whether you give up somewhere along the way or actually finish your book.

This problem will not arise in the first flush of enthu-siasm. Fired with excitement about the characters who have taken hold of you, and the germ of your idea, you may not realise as you begin to scribble the opening pages with that fanatical gleam in your eye that it might take months – even years – to complete your novel. People who have never written a novel do not appreciate the amount of sustained effort which is involved in keeping the idea fresh and interesting, the characters and plot developing satisfac-torily and the flow of the narrative going, over a long period when there will be ups and downs, family and work and world crises, times when your mood will be high or low, or you might even have decided you don't want to bother being a novelist at all.

Deal with difficulties as and when they occur. Give your-self every advantage though – even allowing yourself a good luck talisman if you feel this helps you stand a better chance of ploughing steadily on to the end without being disturbed too drastically by the activity outside the little world that makes up your own particular creative corner.

In the sheer mass of words and pages that make up your novel, it is easy to feel, particularly in the middle of the book when you have lost the impetus of the beginning and you can't seem to see the end at all, that you are getting nowhere. Many novels are abandoned half-way out of sheer discouragement and a sense of inadequacy and frustration. One of the things which make novel-writing different from writing short stories or articles is the fact that it takes such a long time before you see any result, in practical terms, from all your labours.

You might have been struggling with the novel for months but still you have no manuscript to show publishers, no completed work to give you a smug sense of achievement; and the uncertainty of what will emerge from the last, as yet unwritten, section of your book haunts you at nights when you can't sleep and brood about being a failure as a novelist. You can't really share your worries with friends. Even if they are writing novels themselves they will be having different problems, since every novel and every novelist is individual. It is impossible to detail a tricky situation you're encountering in the book to other people, as they don't know what the rest of the plot is about and it is a bad mistake to try and condense the action of a whole book into a few sentences. If you do this, the plot will sound even worse than you thought it was.

Such discouragement and steady dwindling of confidence is not 'artistic temperament' or a sign you are becoming neurotic about your work. The more doubts you suffer from, in fact, the better your writing is likely to be. Writers who never have to worry because they have everything under control and they know all the answers are highly unlikely to produce anything startlingly original or worthwhile.

Emily Bronte, whom we might have imagined to be one of the most level headed of people, secure in an awareness of her own genius, scribbled on one of her poems:

I am more terrifically and idiotically and brutally STUPID than ever I was in the whole course of my incarnate existence. The above precious lines are the fruits of one hour's most agonising labour between $\frac{1}{2}$ past 6 and $\frac{1}{2}$ past 7 in the evening of July – 1836.

Even novelists who have written successful novels already are not immune to self-doubt and uncertainty about the quality of their work. The reason why they do not talk about it as much as beginner writers is because they accept it as an occupational hazard and have learned to overcome it through some of the tricks and pointers included in this chapter. So far as I know, it never actually goes away, even with shelves of published books to give the writer confidence. I still have the same sinking feeling, at some stage along the way, that I have had with every novel I have written.

Hints To Encourage You To Keep Writing

1. The first practical step when you undertake to write a novel is to create some sort of routine for your work. Writing will take quite a lot of time and energy, though there is no rule for exactly how much, for this will vary with every novelist.

Nobody can advise you on how long it ought to take you to complete your book. If I mentioned that the ideal length of time was a year (which was what it took me to complete my first novel), you might be very disconcerted because you'd almost finished after only three weeks. If, on the other hand, I said that my last novel was written in five weeks (which it was) you might feel there was something very wrong if, after eighteen months, you were still labouring away and had only reached page 127.

Take your own time and avoid any sort of pressure, except the pressure you put on yourself to continue to make a decent job of the book, and complete it.

The novelist Georges Simenon is said to have written each of his books in the space of three weeks; he had a rigorous training routine to get him in peak condition. You may be as fast a worker as this, but it's more likely that you will take anything between five or six months and two years to complete your novel. When you start your task therefore, you need to be sure that, for instance, the family is not about to emigrate very shortly, or you're not planning to get married next week.

If possible, make sure you ave a chance to write every day. You may not always be able to write much – a novelist needs 'thinking time' as well as 'writing time' – but you won't get very far with this routine of yours if there is no opportunity to work except on alternate Fridays. And try to use your writing hours for either the actual story itself or something more routine like checking facts, finding out information you need, or tidying your papers and keeping the text of the manuscript up to date. Do not fritter your writing time away on crossword puzzles or throwing paper darts into the coffee mug. Even if you can't actually write anything that day, use your writing time for something which will help your writing.

2. The length of your novel will give you several milestones to chalk up en route. Unless a novelist is very experienced, it is usually difficult to be able to complete a novel to a certain number of words (as one can do more easily with a short story) and you are more than likely to have only the vaguest idea of what the actual length of the finished book will be. The length you are aiming at will probably be determined to a certain extent by the nature of the book; and indeed certain types of novels are required by publishers to be of a certain length. Even if a new novelist feels unable to predict with any confidence that he or she is writing 'a novel of 55,000 words', or even the number of chapters the book will contain, however, the completion of each chapter itself is an achievement. (For practical details on calculating the length of a manuscript and working out the structure of your book; see Chapter 11)

3. You have to be your own boss as well as the workforce when you are writing your novel. Nobody will thunder at you if you don't meet the deadline, or threaten you with dismissal if you have not sorted the whole middle section out and PUT IT ON MY DESK BY MONDAY LUNCH-TIME! It is quite easy simply to avoid doing any work for whatever reason, whether because it seems too much of an effort or because you are dismally certain the whole thing is hopeless. Some would-be novelists have long since stopped actually writing, but live for years in a glorious status quo

where they are 'still working at it, old boy, but I haven't finished the research yet – just contacted the Louvre and a couple of US universities. Got to get it right, you know.'

People who research their novels, people who make notes about their novels, people who talk about their novels and describe them and go into detail about them – no matter how wonderful the research or the notes or the descriptions might be, until they *write* their novels, these people are not novelists.

You have to train your own personal 'boss' to deal with your inner workforce when it's being obstreperous and refusing to settle down to the next chapter. This method we call *Overcoming Laziness by Employing Self-Discipline*.

When your workforce is feeling uncertain, tired of struggling, at a low ebb with regard to self-confidence, your boss should be more generous. In the same way that a carrot may tempt a donkey along a path it does not want to take, small treats will tempt the flagging novelist onward and encourage the workforce to keep on writing. To a novelist, the choicest tit-bit is often an easy section of the book which can be quickly written and turns out so well it needs no revision. Try to award yourself treats and encouragement.

Include in what you write a character or a setting of which you are particularly fond, and while not permitting yourself to wallow in self-indulgence – taking ten pages to describe the sexual charms of your rugged hero or the night of bliss between Maxwell and his nineteen-year-old stepmother, for instance – let yourself go and tell yourself that writing is fun! So often the 'fun' in writing a novel may prove of the masochistic sort, resulting in haggard eyes and sunken cheeks and nights spent worrying about whether details are correct, whether the plot will work out, whether the whole thing is worth the trouble.

Give yourself all the assistance you can as you progress further into your novel. That includes all the good-luck-bringers you want on your desk, your own small rituals as you sit down to write, and a firm but sympathetic inner boss who is there to make sure this novel gets finished, and that it is good.

11
STRUCTURE

WITH all the planning and preparation in the world, all the working out of your intended plot (though many new novelists, or even experienced ones, do little formal planning on paper), it is not until you have been writing for some time that the structure of your book will begin to make itself clear to you.

As with characters and the plot itself, you cannot impose a rigid shape and framework of chapters onto your brain-child, your dream, and expect that as you start to capture that dream and pin it down on paper, it will fit comfortably into the framework you had in mind. Each novel has its own structure – sometimes a structure you have to invent specially in order to tell a particular story. Chapters may need to be longer or shorter than you had planned – you cannot bring your scene abruptly to a close as Roz is opening her mouth to have hysterics, simply because you've come to the bottom of page 40 and every chapter has to be ten pages long.

If it helps to give yourself rules, to plan for chapters of the same length and tell yourself they have to be so many pages long, this is fine; but never be afraid to bend or even break your rules if the story demands that you do so. The power of your narrative and the effect you want to produce for the reader are far more important than neatness. Every novel is a one-off and cannot be duplicated. It is unique, an artistic creation in its own right and as such it needs to find its own individual shape and form.

THE LENGTH OF YOUR BOOK

How does one calculate how many words the book will

contain, or how many words have been written so far. This is done by estimating roughly how many words you write or type per page and multiplying that by the number of pages you have written, or the number of pages you need to complete – unless of course you possess a wonderfully competent computer which will tell *you* how many words it has printed in the course of your novel.

Take a few pages of your book, either written in your handwriting or typed up in the same way you normally complete a page, and count up the number of lines on each page. Take a sample of possibly ten pages, so you can work out your average number of lines per page. Take twenty lines at random from your text and count up the number of words in each line. Your average here will give you roughly how many words you have written per line. Multiplying the number of words per line by the number of lines per page will give you an estimated number of words for each page you write. If you multiply this by either the number of pages already completed or a suitable number to bring the total to the length you want the book to be, your questions about chapter and book length can be answered.

Some people wonder whether they should count every word of a novel individually, since of course the words you write on every page will vary – and what about those blank half-pages where you finished a chapter and started the next on a new sheet of paper? Or the lines of dialogue with just a few words in each line?

No publisher in his right mind would ever expect you to do this. So long as your estimated words per line and lines per page do not vary too erratically, so that you are losing or gaining quite a large number of words compared with your estimated number of words per page – which can make a difference of several thousands of words when you multiply this by several hundred pages for your complete text – it will probably be accurate to within a few hundred words, and that is all a publisher will reasonably expect.

If you are writing a book where the publisher's demands about length are very strict, it is always better to over-run rather than make the book too short. A good editor can easily cut a long manuscript, and your novel might even benefit from cutting, but it is almost impossible to add to a novel that is not long enough unless what is added is 'padding', unnecessary waffling which the competent novelist avoids at all costs.

How long should your book be? This question, along with others like How much should I write each day? or How can I tell whether my plot will work? is very much in the same category as How long is a piece of string? or Why did the chicken cross the road?

New writers who expect clear-cut answers, simple rules they can follow in order to produce a good novel, will search vainly for such blueprints to success because even the acknowledged experts in the novel-writing game, when proffering their own helpful hints, are relying only on the experience of years actually *doing* the writing. And every artist works in his or her own way.

Thus, though Anthony Trollope declared that 'Three hours a day will produce as much as a man ought to write', this cannot really be taken as any sort of guideline. If you are one of the people who write best in eight-hour overnight stints, it would be stupid to set your alarm for three hours and then pack up and go to bed. Similarly, if you can only write for an hour each day – and some people are lucky if they can keep their inspiration going that long – you would be doing yourself harm if you started worrying because you couldn't follow Trollope's advice.

In the same way there is no rule which says a novel has to be of a certain length with new chapters every so many pages. The only rules you need to be aware of are those which publishers keep to when they are deciding whether to buy a novel or not.

With regard to the preferred length of novels, this varies, as titles do, according to changes in fashion and economics of publishing. At one time, for instance, it was quite common for extremely short novels – the type referred to as 'novellas', of anything from 20,000 to 40,000 words long – to be enthusiastically seized on by publishers. Literary novellas appeared alongside 'slim volumes' of verse. Now, though, you would be highly unlikely to interest a publisher in a 'literary novella' or anything else, under 40,000 words at the very least.

The average length for romances, thrillers and other category and genre books today is between 45,000 and 60,000 words, depending on the demands of each publisher and allowing for the fact that you may write some brilliant novel which cannot be confined by rules. (Fuller definitions and further details of category and genre books, and what the publishers expect of them, can be found in Part IV, *The Genre Novel*)

Unless you are planning to write an epic or a saga, though, you would be wise to aim at a length of about 60,000 to 70,000 words. Epics and sagas can be anything up to or even over 100,000 words long, but bear in mind that this is a lot of writing and also that publishers would have to be very certain that any book of this length would sell before they invested money in it. Keep your aspirations modest unless you just *know* your epic is in the same class as Michener's *Hawaii* or Leon Uris' *Exodus*.

THE SHAPE OF YOUR BOOK

Traditionally, novels are divided into chapters, parts, sections or other fragmentary pieces of the whole. In the early days of English fiction, novels appeared disguised as something else – the first modern English novel, *Pamela* by Samuel Richardson, being in the form of letters. Letters, diaries and other methods of putting the story across, such as those used by Stephen King in *Carrie* – newspaper quotes, extracts from books, apparently authentic documents interspersed with the narrative – are employed partly to provide variety for the reader and to break the intensity of the drama as it unfolds, but mainly to persuade readers that the story is *real*. Once readers begin to think: 'Well, all these characters are only a figment of the writer's imagination anyway, so what am I worrying about them for?' the credibility and authenticity of the whole thing is lost.

When you begin to plan the shape of your book, do not

assume you have to split the story into chapters because this is what is usually done. *Use* the shape you give your novel to assist in the illusions you want to create for your readers. Let the chapters or the sections or the parts into which you split the book do more than just give the readers a break – make them work for you. Let them help your readers to accept and believe in your story; let them help you, as the author, to write it convincingly and well.

The most simple structure of a novel is a straightforward chronological account of events, which uses chapter breaks to give the reader a chance to catch his breath, as it were, and to provide the novelist with an opportunity to pick up the story in another part of the field, or after a lapse of time.

Sometimes, however, the novelist may set the whole thing in retrospect, so that the narrator is recalling events which have led up to the present situation, or recounting a happening which occurred entirely in the past. If you use a method like this, avoid dark hints of the: 'Little did we know then' or 'If only we had realised at the time' sort, as these can sound melodramatic and destroy the serious effect you wanted to put across.

Retrospective novels are sometimes told by one character to another – the main body of *Wuthering Heights* is a good example of this. Various techniques are used in *Wuthering Heights*, as well as the tales of the two narrators, to put the story over; diary notes in an old book illustrate the heroine's thoughts and feelings at the time she wrote them, for instance.

If you decide your story can best be told in retrospect, remember you may need to resort to a lot of technical tricks to bring the various scenes to life convincingly. Characters can tell their own bits of the story, old documents can be used as 'evidence' in your novel, letters supposed to have been written in the past can be incorporated. But even so, if the novel is set in the present, you will need a good strong framework for the present-day characters to exist in, and your readers will need to find this framework credible. The sort of set-up where the young heroine is hired to classify papers and documents at a country house, and as well as falling for her saturnine employer, begins to become involved in the events of the past as she works each day in the library uncovering evidence, is rather hackneyed now.

You may decide to tell your story in the form of letters or a diary, each of which gives you a comforting sense of familiarity with the form and makes it easy to be able to pick up the thread again whenever you have stopped writing for a while. These too have their drawbacks, though, for they are necessarily limited to a first person viewpoint unless letters from a lot of different people are included. The modern trend is rather biased against letters or a diary form and unless you think it would be impossible to tell your story any other way, you would probably be better to avoid them.

Since books are structured in layers, as it were, you may decide your novel would work best like this. A very popular framework is that of a 'journey' which portrays the main character undertaking a journey of some sort – either physical or mental – in the present.

Interspersed with accounts of the journey, another narrative may run alongside detailing the events which led up to it, but posing unresolved questions which will only be answered when past and present have been reconciled at the journey's end.

Setting a book in several periods of time as you tell your story can also be usefully used for deep and probing studies in relationships. Perhaps the readers see your heroine sometimes as a happy and laughing child; part of the time she is a disillusioned and bitter young woman. From such mosaic pictures a moving and complete portrait can be built up.

It is also possible to use different periods of time in addition to different sets of characters, though you will need to be certain that you know exactly what you are doing if you employ such a complicated mechanism for telling your tale, or the whole thing could end up as a jumbled mass which means nothing at all to your readers. Study the brilliant *Red Shift* by Alan Garner if you find this sort of approach exciting.

You can split your novel into sections in order to present a picture of your main protagonist, and let each section be told from the viewpoint of a different character, so that the first person narrator changes in each section. This is a method that has been used very successfully in the past when novelists wanted to give a rounded portrait of some historical figure. Two very good examples are Norah Lofts' *The Lute-Player* and Martha Rofheart's *Cry 'God for Harry'*.

A complex structure means you have lifelines to cling to as you write. By knowing what you are doing to gain your effects as you manipulate the structure of your story you will avoid becoming bogged down in difficult emotional sections of your novel. Thus, switching from one character to another, or from some scene in the past to your hero's current 'journey'– whether this is taking place in a seat in a darkened plane as your hero wings onwards through the night to his destination, or in a darkened hospital bed as he waits for the morning and wrestles with his soul – in these and other such cases, the awareness of employing crafts-manship and technical skill gives the writer a certain detachment from the emotions of his characters.

Furthermore, if there is some sort of framework laid down to guide you as you proceed, you are never faced with the agonising question of: 'Well, where do I go from here?' which can beset even experienced writers.

The main drawback of a complex framework for any novel is that, unless you are careful, the structure itself – something positive and real, which can be noted down on sheets of paper so that it looks impressive and proves you are making progress – will become the most important thing in your book. Structure can never take the place of what the novel should actually say to the reader, however skilfully or interestingly you might have planned it.

In addition, though readers are always fascinated by clever twists and elaborately built-up puzzles, novelties which depart from the ordinary chronological order of events, they will quickly tire if there is no real meat in what you have written, no message or theme, no worthwhile characters they can identify with and concern themselves about, no story progressing towards a satisfactory end.

The process of writing a novel is similar to the process of unearthing archaeological treasures from the ground. The archaeologist, by carefully removing the dust and grime and debris of ages, reveals the treasure in all its glory to the spectator's interested gaze. The novelist, in a similar manner, does not actually invent his novel – make a working model from sketches, test it to see if it functions successfully and then rush off to patent it. Rather, he frees it from the clutter of extra wordage and superfluous detail and excess thought that is buzzing round in his head. The precious object revealed is what is important in each case, not the clever and complicated methods used to make it available to the public.

THE CONTENT OF YOUR BOOK

Whatever else your book is about, there are certain basic elements it must contain or it will not work as a novel. We have already seen that a novel must not be static, it has to move forward (or backward!) and progress towards some sort of climax or resolution.

In fact, a novel consists quite simply of the presentation of a problem or conflict which will involve your main character or characters in some sort of struggle. At strategic points throughout the narrative, climaxes must occur which mark either partial triumphs or defeats, or the revelation of further complications arising from the basic struggle. Sub-plots and secondary plots run alongside your main conflict and provide lesser struggles for some of your secondary characters, often underlining the main conflict or overlapping with it. By the end of the novel, the threads of all these conflicts must work themselves through and be resolved to the reader's satisfaction, even if the ending is not what he was anticipating or hoping for.

By the end of your novel, this particular story must be told. Maybe another conflict has taken the place of the first, but that belongs in another book – if you ever decide to write it. Each novel's struggle must be contained within its own particular volume.

The conflict or struggle in a novel can be of any sort. It can be social, involving the wars of a nation or nations, and how these affect your main characters. Will they survive? Will things ever be the same after this? Will they ever forgive their enemies after what they have seen? Can they hold onto snatched happiness in the middle of all the horror or will that too be dashed away?

Problems involving survival and all its attendant smaller struggles provide for endless plots based around conflict with the status quo. Other struggles of this nature, not necessarily involving war, have produced stories where the main characters have to trek to safety from crashed planes in the middle of a jungle, up a mountain or even in the Arctic Circle.

Some useful background where the conflict is partly physical – will they freeze to death? Will the crocodiles get them if the raft sinks? – can give you structural elements to include in the framework of your story, but remember that if this is a novel, a simple account of the journey across the glaring desert sands to safety is not enough. There has to be some further conflict of character, some interaction between the people involved in your story, or else you are writing what should have been a non-fiction book: an essay or an account of your theory about How to Cross a Desert.

Your characters cannot exist each within a vacuum. It is possible to have a novel with only a few characters involved, or even with only one, but in this case the conflict would have to be between that person's isolation and his/her memories of past relationships or longing for new ones.

You can have conflicts between your characters and their environment, between them and other people, within the group; or within themselves between their desires and their conscience, between love and duty, between their religious beliefs and their doubts. Lists have been made from time to time about the different sorts of conflicts a writer can incorporate into a novel –between man and man, man and animal, man and woman, man and nature, man and God. You could add to that any others you think of, man and society, for instance; or man and machine, where the hero is obsessed with motor racing or is involved in a duel-to-the-death with his computer.

Here again, though, it is not the length of the list that matters. Conflict is everywhere, and one of the most basic struggles depicted in novels is still that of a heroine who wants to believe that true love and a knight on a white charger will one day come her way, but is convinced that in the everyday world this is too much to expect. It can take the hero almost the whole book to persuade her to stop fighting and accept that he is the answer to her romantic dreams.

Without conflict, without struggle, there is no story to tell. Your hero, having crashed in the wilds of Alaska, produces up-to-the-minute survival gear, radios for assistance and within a few hours is being winched up by a helicopter. No problem – but no story.

Girl meets Boy; they realise they were meant for each other and, in two pages, are in each other's arms behind the potted palms in the conservatory or the strobe lights at the disco. All very well, but now you have no novel left to write – unless something or somebody is going to place obstacles in the way of this perfect love story. Since they have already committed themselves, however, readers will feel the most exciting part of the novel is over.

By presenting the final climax first – or revealing too soon what eventually resulted from the struggle or the conflict, you can kill your novel stone dead. Once the questions posed by the opening chapters of your book have been answered in the minds of the readers, they will feel uneasy and restless if the book continues to unfold. Readers can sense when a story has reached its natural end, even if they cannot explain *why* they feel something is missing after this point has been passed.

Badly written novels can 'end' very early on in the narrative, but because the novelist is not aware he has answered all the questions, made all the explanations, left nothing more for the readers to discover about the outcome of the story's conflicts, he continues to write. What he writes for the rest of the book is probably 'padding', detail and incident which is unimportant or repetitive and which adds nothing to the effect on his readers nor tells them anything of relevance.

It is even possible for a confused and uncertain writer who is not aware of what a novel actually *is*, to come to a natural 'end' more than once. The resulting narrative will be patchy and disjointed because each time an 'ending' is reached, some unrelated thread or line of action involving characters who have previously played no part in the story may have to be taken up in order for the writer to be able to continue.

Whether or not your story is told in retrospect, make sure that you never reach a point where – without intending to do it – you have said everything, and can add no more which you could honestly claim was necessary and relevant. Always keep the most important and significant information back so that there is still no complete answer to the questions the reader has been asking himself.

If, for instance, the story starts as an operation is in progress with the hero's life in the balance, and the narrator then recalls the events which have led to this traumatic moment, do not reveal right until the end of the book whether the operation has actually been successful if that is the crucial point of the whole story. Do not make the mistake of 'ending' your book half-way down page 2 when the surgeon pronounces that he's out of danger, and then devoting the rest of the narrative to explaining exactly how your hero came to have the accident, how he'd always had a fear of flying but was determined to overcome it so took flying lessons and eventually got a job as a pilot.

If readers already know the most important thing, that he will live they will not really care that his dedicated effort to overcoming his fear nearly wrecked his marriage, so that in the end, he sold his own plane to buy a luxury villa in Spain and devote himself to his wife, and that it was on their flight out – as passengers – that the crash occurred. All of this has become just background detail and has no pulling power to keep readers glued to page after page throughout thirty chapters.

If the bride and groom are waiting at the altar on page one of your novel, glaring and looking as if they could tear each other to pieces, and you take the story right back to their meeting in the springtime in Vienna and follow the progress of their love affair through fights and business rivalries, make sure you save *right for the end* the triumphant information that they *are not marrying each other*. This is a double wedding, and when their own respective groom and bride take their arms, old feuds are forgotten and the past gives way to the happiness of the present.

12
A MIRROR TO NATURE?

SHAKESPEARE'S famous advice to the players in *Hamlet* is often quoted and misquoted when people begin to try and define the nature of art, whether it is writing, painting, acting, music, sculpture.

The purpose of art, it is claimed, is to hold a 'mirror up to nature'. If you are writing a novel, this theory can cause a lot of confusion, as it suggests that what the novelist has to do is faithfully to represent real life within his pages.

In fact, nothing could be further from the truth. If you did attempt to make a faithful copy of a slice of reality, it would never work as a novel – and probably not as anything else either. We have already seen that most of the effects in a novel are achieved by artificial means. They do not 'just happen' because that particular novelist is a genius.

As you progress and become aware of more of the skills and techniques of novel-writing, you will see that *all fiction is completely unreal*. There is nothing in a novel which is actually true-to-life – any sense of reality is an illusion created in the minds of the readers.

The better a novelist you are, the more 'real' people will think your work is; the harder you have worked to create your illusions, the more effortless everything will appear. Sheridan (although not a novelist) said truthfully:

> You write with ease to show your breeding
> But easy writing curst hard reading.

Alexander Pope commented:

> True ease in writing comes from art, not chance,
> As those move easiest who have learned to dance.

Samuel Johnson declared: 'What is written without

effort is in general read without pleasure.'

Everything in your novel should give the impression that it is spontaneous. For the reader your book has no past history, no previous existence in untidy manuscript pages on the floor of your spare room, no nail-biting months being read by a publisher. When a reader lifts the cover of your novel, turns to the first page and starts to read, each movement, speech and incident in the story is fresh and new, everything is happening for the first time. The reader should be caught up in the immediacy of the situation, unable to stop reading in case the hero makes the wrong decision, willing him not to.

In order to create this 'real' effect the novelist has to be very selective over everything which goes into his novel, in much the same way that a good cook chooses the ingredients for a dish with care.

We have seen that life, the structure of society, the way people behave, the way relationships can develop or deteriorate, the things people say, the things they don't say, are all so much raw material for your novel. But the sum total of your own awareness, the material you have at your fingertips *from simply being alive and alert yourself* is far too great to include everything even if you wrote a hundred novels. And so, when planning how to proceed, how the story will go, how it should build up in intensity from an intriguing beginning to a gripping climax at the end, you must be very aware of the artificiality of the work you are doing, and select every incident, every scene and every conversation with care.

'Drama,'claimed Alfred Hitchcock, 'is life with the dull bits left out.' And another great film director, Jean Renoir, commented: 'Reality may be very interesting but a work of art must be a creation.'

Strangely, many new writers feel confined within the bounds of what they themselves have experienced. When planning plots, they use situations and incidents only in the way in which these have worked out for them. Remember when writing fiction that you are not making a confession. You can distort the truth, change the endings of incidents which actually happened to you or to someone you know, and lie blatantly without fear or shame.

All fiction is a lie. Your novel is going to be one big falsehood, which you must persuade your readers to swallow. Contrary to the popular belief that a novelist's main requirement is a good imagination, the most useful skills he can cultivate in this direction are those of the fluent liar and convincing con-man.

Take from your experience, or the experience of others whom you know, only the bits and pieces which will add significance to your story. Do not try to include whole incidents from life, for instance. Do not attempt to include the complete course run by relationships which you have witnessed and know to be true.

Learn to select, to take just the relevant scenes and incidents – or parts of them – that you need. Do not feel obliged to 'tell it as it happened', if this means the story suffers and the readers have to wade through a great deal of repetitive and consequently ineffective material.

If you were writing about the problems of a woman whose husband was an alcoholic, for instance, or a woman whose husband beat her, you might have personal knowledge of such cases and want to make sure the full details were included in your novel so that readers would realise just how terrible the sufferings of your heroine were. In addition you might feel that since you possessed all this personal insight and experience, you wanted to make the fullest use of it, so your novel would be written at great length, including all the small details and incidents you could think of.

In fact, 'telling it all as it is' achieves exactly the opposite effect to the one you are seeking. Since fiction is so artificial, points only have to be made *once* in a story, illustrated *once* with a relevant scene, conversation or incident. Just *one* dreadful clash between your heroine and her husband, following on some smaller details preparing the way for this climax, will be enough to distress and shock readers and alert them to her painful situation.

If you were to follow this, grimly determined to make sure the readers are fully aware of the situation, with a second scene where he beats her again, it would establish only that the violence was on-going, something everyday in her life. It would not have the horrific impact of the previous scene.

A third similar incident would be too much for fiction to take unless some new element were added, such as the plans she might be making for escape and freedom, or her attempts to fight back, or the intervention of another character.

Repetition does not make the points you want to underline about your characters or their relationships come over to the readers with more force, unless the story is being written in a style which is using the repetition of words or phrases – or even incidents – for effect.

It is significant that the effects you *can* create with repetition are those of boredom, monotony, frustration. Take a story about travellers lost in the desert. The style in which you write the account of their wanderings might be condensed to staccato phrases:

> Sand, No water. Can't drink sand. Must have water. We seem to have been walking for miles – blisters on our feet, tongues going black – Got to have water. Oh, God, the burning sand. Everywhere this sand. Must find water.

Even this highly dramatic version of events should not go on for too long, or else the readers will lose interest in the monotonous cry for water, yawn and put the book down, leaving the hero and his party still searching for their oasis.

If you think about the horrors chronicled on television news as a matter of course – something we accept as a part of everyday life – you will see how repetition can dull the impact of even the most shocking stories. And even though you are writing fiction, you should bear in mind the old journalistic adage that 'MILLIONS DROWN IN INDIA is a disaster; LOCAL TODDLER DROWNS IN VILLAGE

POND is *news*'.

Everything is relative when you are constructing your novel. Maybe you could have detailed twenty scenes between your heroine and her brutal husband, all of them different. The readers don't need them. They've got the message after they've seen him break the whisky bottle over her head and set fire to her hair the first time. They want action: either he must get his come-uppance or she has to get away from him. They are ready and waiting for your story to gather itself together, for you to set the pace and the mood and plunge right into the conflict and the drama.

Even if your novel is more personal and introspective, and will chronicle her gradual awareness of her husband's sufferings, so that in the end they are trying to fight his problem together, do not over-do the accounts of the times he promised he would never touch another drop and then came crashing into her room drunk. Remember the hero of the desert and his oasis. Don't make your book monotonous.

Because a novel has to convince the reader it is real and the story is completely credible, the things that happen in real life have to be severely vetted before they can be included as part of your story.

Real life is frequently unbelievable, amazing, incredible and highly unlikely. Coincidences in real life occur all the time; people actually *do* travel thousands of miles for a holiday and find themselves in the same hotel as 'that snooty couple from next door'! People actually *do* discover long-lost treasure worth millions while digging their garden. People actually *do* meet their brother/sister with whom they've lost touch for forty years, when a neighbour sees a small item in the newspaper and recognises the name.

Real life, in fact, breaks all the rules of fiction in a quite incredible manner. If such occurrences were in a novel, they would be thrown out immediately as 'too unbelievable to be true'. This is why the novelist has to work hard for that effect of artless realism.

Coincidence in a story will much weaken it. Readers have their own instinctive set of rules about what they will and will not allow in a novel – that is, unless the novelist is so brilliant that he can just string any old sentence or two together, any old way, and the readers are so utterly dazzled that they hang onto every syllable, their critical faculties for the time being completely suspended. There are writers with this gift. I am not one of them. It is more than likely that you are not one of them either. We have to assume we are going to have to follow the Readers' Code in novels we write, in order that our books will impress them as being in every respect 'true to life'. In other words our books will have to be skilfully crafted to give that impression.

The Readers' Code (compared with real life)

1. Stories and plots must not depend on coincidence or the intervention of outside forces which have no part to play in the conflict/struggle you are detailing. All the solutions to problems (within reason) must arise from the activities in the early part of the narrative or else the efforts made by your characters.

REAL LIFE: Coincidence takes place; chance meetings with complete strangers whom one never sees again can result in successful applications for a job or have some other desired effect; people may interfere in the lives of others and the resulting muddle prove such a shambles there is no way to sort it out. Real life contains far too many unresolved questions on every level to make for a good, believable plot.

2. Characters must be consistent. They must not do things which are inexplicable. Everything they do must spring from what we have previously seen as part of their personality, even if this new departure seems a surprise. They must not behave irrationally unless they are some sort of eccentric or just about to give way to the stress of their situation.

REAL LIFE: All characters in real life are inconsistent, irrational, unpredictable. It would be impossible to fit them into the framework of any book unless they had been 'fictionalised' beforehand. Fictional characters are very much simpler and easier to understand.

3. The reader does not enjoy situations where control seems to have been taken from the characters with whom he is identifying. This *can* work in cases where the principal character is at the mercy of the elements or a natural disaster – a landslide, an avalanche, fire or extreme cold. In such cases, the readers will identify with the main character's efforts to fight and combat the disaster.

Situations where the main character is held a helpless victim by the senseless inhumanity of man rather than by nature (which readers accept to have its own laws), can be very difficult to handle. If your principal character is tortured, brutalised, beaten, raped or otherwise made dependent on the whim of a crazed or sadistic person to whom it is impossible to appeal, and from whom normal human compassion is obviously not to be expected, this will distress the average reader (apart from those who indulge vicariously in such displays of brutishness as a form of compensation).

The reason for this distress is not purely because the situation might be an upsetting one, but because control here is out of the hands of the main character and in the hands of someone who probably seems – or should seem – sub-human or abnormal to the extent that no ordinary communication can be made with them. The result is a sense of helplessness and a feeling that nothing can be done. All novels are about some sort of struggle; but when, for whatever reason, the struggle has to be given up or abandoned or held in abeyance while the main character cowers and is unable to take any action for fear of unreasonable reprisals, readers share this sick sense of helpless fear and anger. It is not a pleasant feeling.

Even in books about war where the main characters are tortured, it is important to set this in the context of activity in the story before and after. Never let your novel stagnate while the powers of evil – in whatever form – rule. Never take from your main character the ability to at least think revolutionary thoughts, even if he or she is unable for the time being to put them into practice.

REAL LIFE: Real life can be so unbearable in this respect that we can understand the reader's desire for a sense of order, a sense of method and significance. In real life, there is not necessarily fair play or justice. Heroes who hold out to their last gasp do not somehow rally and then save the situation with a superhuman effort. There is no discrimination in unpleasantness and suffering, pain and grief. The blow could fall at any time, without warning, on any one of us.

So it is the duty of the novelist to provide the reader under this section of the Code with the hope and inspiration he is seeking. Be realistic but be careful as you handle torment and suffering – remember there is more than enough of it in your reader's life already.

William Faulkner declared that 'It is the writer's privilege to help man endure by lifting his heart.' And he wasn't just talking about the authors of paperback romance.*

---

*Two novels in which violence and the effects of being 'outside the law' in the accepted sense are explored by master storytellers, are William Golding's *Lord of the Flies* and *A High Wind in Jamaica* by Richard Hughes.

SECOND INTERLUDE
SECOND CHECK LIST

CATCHING up on the main points which have been made in the last few chapters, here is a resume of suggestions and information, with more hints to assist you in the central section of your novel:

1. Unless you chance upon some unexpectedly brilliant and apposite title, give your novel a 'working title' for convenience and don't waste too much time worrying about it. Be aware of fashions and trends when you are considering the final title for your book.

2. Humour any superstitious whims you may develop about your work, so long as these do not interfere with the actual writing process. Do not try to write under circumstances which you find impossibly distracting or difficult to cope with. Be as comfortable as possible, both physically and mentally, when you sit down to work.

3. Do not try to write when you are feeling ill, upset or very tired. But if you find that it's only when you are dropping with exhaustion that you can plunge into your novel, obviously you know yourself best and must work in the way that is easiest for you.

The average writer will probably be frustrated and fretful if tiredness or preoccupation with outside problems is blocking the flow of his or her book. You may even feel you will never be able to write another word, and get into a panic.

In such cases, try to get away from the book. Forget it

for a few hours at least, blank it out. Have a good rest. Try to allow yourself a breathing space before you return, hopefully refreshed, to the fray. This is not always easy to do, as the temptation is to struggle on with whatever problem of construction or character is bothering you, and gnaw away at it as a dog does with a bone. But you will never write your best when tired and dispirited. Call in your own personal boss and get those workers of yours out for a brisk walk or order them to bed for an early night.

4. Overcome the state commonly referred to as WRITER'S BLOCK, where it seems you are up against a blank wall as regards your novel and will never be able to proceed any further with it, by a sideways, crab-like method of progress. If you cannot think of ways to carry on with that particular chapter, if your mind is blank about further developments, if you have simply come to a standstill, then approach your work from an altogether different direction.

Skip the incident or incidents you were planning, go to another character and let him or her take the action forward, consciously alter your style, allow yourself to dwell on something which might seem trivial – the way a garden looked that day. Let the story pick up *after* the scene you were trying so hard to describe; or view that top-level meeting through the eyes of a child watching the cars arrive. Re-educate yourself to *enjoy* what you are writing, rather than just slogging away grimly.

If none of this seems to work, try writing some quite different narrative, or even a poem or an account of the local dramatic society's production or the flower show, anything just to get you back using words easily and into the flow of writing. Or give yourself a week's break, and by the end of that week you will probably be straining at the leash to carry on with your novel.

We must, however, consider the possibility that, horrific though it may seem, your novel might have come to a sticky end. Belly-flopped. Fizzled out. This can and does

100

happen, and it is far better to be realistic about it and make sensible plans to abandon it and start another than to keep on battering vainly at something you know in your secret heart is never going to be any good. Nothing is more soul-destroying than to waste time and energy on a story which has already died on you, and keep trying to force the illusion of life into it, knowing this will never work.

Some novels start off well, but might come to an unexpected and early end far too soon because the plot simply was not strong enough. In others, the development of the characters does not take off in the way you had hoped it would, so that they never really start to live as people. Sometimes there does not seem to be any real reason why the novel comes to a standstill, except that the whole thing begins to look contrived and manufactured, and you can't feel it really matters very much either way whether you continue, since there is no vital spark there.

It is just as foolish to cling determinedly to a fizzled-out book and refuse to give it up as it is to throw up a perfectly good novel as 'hopeless' when with a little application you could have finished it and produced a saleable manuscript. But of course, the problem for beginners is how to know whether a novel with which they are having difficulty has in fact fizzled out, or whether it's just themselves who are suffering from *Writers' Block*.

However many people you might show the manuscript to, whatever advice you may seek, in the long run only you, the novelist, can tell if a novel is worth working on or whether you would be wiser to abandon it.

But remember that it is very hard to keep a good novel down. If you continue to be haunted, tormented, if you feel you can't get away from the characters and the struggle of organising the words, plot, scenes and incidents – then you would be foolish to stop writing.

If you *know* deep within yourself that the reason why this story isn't working out is because it wasn't really good enough, and if you could have started again, you'd have done quite a different sort of story, with a different sort of main character, then for heaven's sake, never mind about

101

the thought of how suitable your first one would be for a TV series, and how it would be ideal for a film – put it aside and get on with the story which interests you because it has living characters and depth, and recognise honestly that you made a mistake. There's nothing wrong in this.

Readers – and indeed the general public as a whole – are largely unaware of the novels which successful novelists do *not* succeed in getting published. Most of these errors of judgement are never talked about. Quite naturally, successful novelists talk only about their success, rarely about their failures. But speaking for myself, I can reveal that for each novel of mine that was published, I wrote certainly one – possibly two – which was dumped and never made the grade.

5. Remember that nothing in writing is ever wasted. Everything you write makes you more fluent, a better writer. All the research and checking, the conscientious spadework and organisation of material, the experience of actually writing, is providing you with the foundations you need. Even material you discard has been necessary as a preliminary to the writing you actually include.

6. Overcome disillusionment with your work and lack of self-confidence (if this should occur) by establishing a brisk and practical working routine, tailored to suit your own particular requirements and commitments. Keep to the routine to give you the impetus to complete your book.

7. Remember that you are your own workforce, boss, market researcher, time-and-motion expert and everything else rolled into one. Keep yourself disciplined so that you don't become diverted by minutiae or tempted to avoid the actual hard graft of writing for the more pleasurable aspects of being considered a 'writer'.

8. Be aware of the structure of your novel and organise the potential length of the book accordingly, bearing in mind also the requirements of publishers.

9. Use the form in which you tell the story – chapters, section etc – to help give credibility to your novel. Choose your method of narration – diary, letters, a retrospective approach, case history or whatever – in the same manner, to add authenticity and aid your effect.

10. Do not allow the framework of your story to become more important than the content of the novel itself.

11. Be aware that each novel consists of a basic conflict or struggle, which has to work itself out within this particular book.

12. Do not give the final answers to the questions posed by your book's conflict/struggle until the end. Remember that once you have answered these questions, you have in effect finished the story, and all the rest of your information is just background detail.

13 Remember that all fiction is artificial and unreal. The effect of 'realism' has to be skilfully created and all the effort hidden from readers. Everything included in a novel should be selected with care to play its own part in the overall effect.

14. Be aware that because fiction is artificial, points only need to be made and illustrated once. Repetition dulls impact.

15. Reality in a story is quite different from 'real life', which is often so unbelievable readers would never accept it.

16. A plot has to be a contained unit, where the developments and solutions arise in a logical manner. Coincidence will weaken a plot.

17. Characters cannot behave irrationally. They have to be

reasonably consistent or readers will find them difficult to accept, even though people in real life are irrational and inconsistent.

18. Do not include scenes of unreasonable violence where the main characters are arbitrarily stripped (whether physically or mentally) of dignity and reduced to simply enduring, all hope and initiative taken from them. Never give readers the impression that there is no sense, order or justice, or allow anarchy to be glorified in what you write.

13
TEAM WORK

I N the final section of your book you will need to deploy your inner workforce carefully so that the many small details which are involved in rounding off a novel are efficiently dealt with.

It is in building up towards the final climax, and the methods you use to tie up loose ends, explain any queries and clear the decks (as it were) to make way for the grand finale, that you will need to be particularly well-organised.

Most new novelists imagine that if they need to be organised at all, it is at the beginning rather than anywhere else. This is understandable because although everybody can imagine what it would be like to begin a novel, even if they never actually do, it is virtually impossible for anyone to conjure up a picture of what it is like to be part or half-way through and heading for the end of a novel, unless they have gone through the experience.

As you proceed and it is becoming obvious that, whether you planned it or not, the end of your book is looming somewhere on the horizon (even if you still have quite a long way to go) you will need to get the workforce organised and briefed on their various missions.

A novelist has to be able to hold two quite opposing attitudes towards his book. On one hand, in order for the readers to be able to identify with the characters he has created, he has to believe in, adore and know his characters with every fibre of his being. What they do and say, the tilt of the heroine's head and the hero's crooked nose that he says he got when boxing, but which was actually the result of falling off the roof must hold more significance for the novelist than any of the stories recounted in the daily paper, or the pronouncements of the prime minister on TV news.

Every novelist must love the characters he is writing about, probably more than he will ever love a real person. He will talk about them as part of his family, as though they might walk through the door any moment. It is impossible to write a good novel about characters you have no interest in.

So one part of your workforce must be active all the way through your novel, cherishing and encouraging your characters onward through the story with the vicarious enjoyment and sense of pride felt by any possessively fond parent. You need to be there right up to the last paragraph, cheering and waving, as it were, involved so deeply that – as many novelists find – the parting of the ways between you and your characters when you reach the end is a great wrench.

On the other hand, however, another part of you must right from the start be cool and aloof, with no emotional response whatsoever to the events you are chronicling. This unit of your workforce has to be calculating, unimpressed by sentimental appeals, unmoved by admiration or pity, absorbed entirely in working out the effects you need to achieve and the best methods to use to get them exactly right.

If either of these sections of the novelist's brain takes over at the expense of the other, the result will be bad. Over-emotionalism will mean that the story turns weak and mushy, and control is lost. The result will probably be melodramatic and boring. But if too much control is exercised and all emotion is disguised tightly behind a too-stiff upper lip there will be no depth to the narrative, it will all be on the surface. This too will be boring because it is so superficial.

In the earlier sections of your book, you establish your characters, state your conflicts, introduce complications, set the ball rolling to put the story in motion. The various threads of plot and sub-plot begin to weave and intertwine.

In the later chapters of your book, as you head for the end, your workforce has to begin the build-up to the final climax. This must be a well-organised affair, not just something you thought about briefly a few pages before you started the last chapter. We have seen that effects in a novel have to be worked at to seem 'real' and spontaneous. Any situation which arises at the end of your book, too, needs to have any relevant 'scenery' or information about it planted in the minds of your readers beforehand, otherwise it will seem as unbelievable as a hand thrusting a missing 'prop' onto the stage.

In real life, things are never there just because there is a need for them. Chairs are not provided, so ordinary people have to stand, or sit on the floor. In novels, it would be highly embarrassing to have to explain that when the detective went out to make that last significant phone call the village louts had vandalised the public call box, so he missed his final clue. Or that your heroine wasn't there to receive her unexpected bouquet of roses because she'd got gastric flu and was suffering in the bathroom so she didn't hear the doorbell.

Everything that is mentioned in a novel, even the things which seem like a drawback– a lift which does not work or a window where the catch has broken – always has to have some bearing on the plot. It is up to your team to smooth the way in advance, so that no practical detail has been forgotten and everything that is mentioned will be there, but so unobtrusively the readers never notice how this sleight-of-hand was done.

If you want your heroine to collapse onto a chaise-longue in the big bust-up at the end of your book, make sure it is perfectly feasible and reasonable for a convenient chaise-longue to be at hand. Don't, for instance, have her collapsing onto a chaise-longue in the kitchen, while slaving over the stove!

Part of your workforce should be busy, as you progress further into your novel, in anticipating items and information for the various scenes you will be describing later. They should introduce information, drop hints which will be taken up further on. They should also be anticipating queries which will be posed by your readers and if possible, answering these in a neat, unobtrusive manner so that by the end of the book, small details are out of the way, little problems which held the attention of the readers for a while have been dealt with, and the big issues which are going to make up the climax can stand alone.

If you do not prepare the ground for an effective ending long before the final chapter, you will have threads left hanging, unresolved bits of plot, niggling queries which will remain for ever unanswered. Try to control the different relationships between characters, and the ways in which sub-plots and secondary stories progress, by explaining small details as things happen instead of giving huge chunks of explanation at the end.

Reveal some of your lesser secrets as the story progresses, answer a few questions at a time as events occur, so that in the final section of your book things are beginning to fall into place and readers can give their full attention to the really important conflict/struggle/clash which marks the final resolution of the novel.

14
THE END

THE fact that a novel has an end is in itself completely artificial and very much removed from life. In real life there are no endings, happy or otherwise. Nothing finishes itself off, ties up the bits and pieces, resolves the conflicts or comes to an emotional standstill – even briefly. So you are dealing with an art form which has to present in a believable manner, a concept which actually does not exist.

The 'happy ending' of romance, so despised by intellectual snobs, is no more and no less unreal than the ending of some gigantic, sprawling creation which roams into metaphysics and explores dimensions in time and space – and it is more than likely that the romantic 'happy ending' will be far more skilfully crafted.

I once read – though I cannot recollect whose view this was – a comment to the effect that a good novel should conduct itself like a good Christian and proceed forward through its life with its death-bed always in mind. Not in any depressing or gloomily prophetic manner, you understand, but with an awareness in the novelist's subconscious right from the start, not of what the ending will be – since this might not be clear – but of the *sort* of ending it will have.

If, for instance, you know when you start Chapter One that the ending of your novel will be very much more deep and tragic than your readers probably suspect as they enjoy the light-hearted scenes in the opening pages, you should (without giving anything away) have an impression, an awareness of your ending always at the back of your brain as you write. Your heroine, bowed in grief as she will be when the crunch comes, but rising to a courage and dignity nobody would ever have thought she possessed, must be there, a silent ghost from the future, haunting those summer scenes of her youth in your opening chapters. If you can feel her presence, however vaguely, you will, without being aware you are doing so, choose the right words which prepare the ground for the woman who will emerge later, and make the ending of your novel not only believable but inevitable.

Inevitability is the quality which will lift your novel above the obvious and the trite. If the readers had hoped that your heroine would rise above her poverty-stricken background and had cheered her every inch of her stubborn and hard-as-nails way across the political arenas of the western world, hoping she'd left that awful slum behind for ever, there would be a sort of poetic justice at the end if she were defeated by her own son, fighting to preserve the heritage of the past in Britain's cities and blocking her bid to raze her own particular slum to the ground.

We have seen that the ending of a novel should spring from the events in earlier chapters, that the whole story should seem to proceed in an inescapable manner to an ending which readers will feel is absolutely the only ending that was right for that novel and those characters. They might feel upset because the ending is not altogether a 'happy' one, and you might even feel upset yourself and wonder whether to be kinder to your hero and heroine.

This is where the delicate balance between a novelist's two opposing attitudes to his book proves its worth, for if you let sentimentality rule your head and provide an unrealistic 'happy' ending when your workforce is pursing its lips disapprovingly and you know very well that you are avoiding the real issue, you will probably find that you have ruined your book and will have to re-write the end.

Most readers, even if they have no idea of it, possess a sense of intuitive truth and an awareness of what is right and proper in the scheme of things. They may be sorry a book ends comparatively sadly, but if the author had attempted to jolly things up a bit by cancelling the executions and letting the hero marry his sweetheart after all, they would have felt not so much sorry as disappointed

110

and indignant. Does this fool who'd seemed such a sensitive writer realise that things don't work out in reality as they do in fairy tales? Why, they'd thought this was going to be such a moving, dignified novel, and the end turned into nothing but a farce!

There has to be a rightness about your ending, a sense that moral laws and judgements have been seen to govern your story and that poetic and other justice has, in however incidental a manner, been seen to be done. This does not mean that nobody ever gets away with anything in fiction, but it explains comments you may have heard – or even made yourself about some particular story like: 'Oh, I was so disappointed, he ended up with the wrong woman', or 'It didn't seem right that he got away'.

Remarks of this nature are not expressions of the moral rectitude of the speaker. They are made from a sense of disquiet about the pattern of events which has been presented, a feeling that something is artistically wrong rather than morally or socially incorrect. Your characters must live out their destinies and you will find, as we saw in earlier chapters, that they are far more aware than their creator of what their rightful destinies should be.

If you ever feel torn between providing an ending that had seemed 'so right' or 'neat' or 'ideal', and some weird and apparently haphazard solutions that your characters seem to want to impose on themselves, you will probably be wisest to let them have their way. Sometimes they might even refuse to go with you as far as you had intended to take them, and will stop in their tracks. I tried for weeks to complete a final chapter for one of my novels, and was becoming quite ill with frustration, when I suddenly realised that the novel had finished at the end of the previous chapter with a speech one of the characters had made. There was nothing left to say, and my characters had seen this, but it took me weeks before the penny dropped.

So it is desirable – even necessary – for your novel to have some sense of inevitability about the end, so that readers nod sagely and comment to each other that of course, the story had to finish like that, there was no other way it *could* have ended really. Even though it seemed as though there was going to be a tender romance, one knew right from the start if one thought about it that John would *never* be able to cope with domesticity, he was so spiritual, unworldly almost, I mean it just wouldn't have been *right* if he'd married her, and it would never have worked, and I think she knew all the time she was going to lose him, that was why she tried to cage him and keep him …(and so on).

This does not mean, though, that your story should be predictable.

If your novel is predictable, it is bad. If the readers are yawning half-way through because they can see the ending trundling along miles away in full view of everybody, and there isn't a single surprise on the way there, this is not the stuff of which good books are made. If everything that happens is contrived and so obvious that you can practically hear the characters say : 'Oh, how fortunate, I needed to make an urgent call to London so wasn't it lucky that we chanced across this native village and found there was an Englishman living here whose hut contains powerful radio equipment' or 'Heavens, the submarine has made its way up the river and is surfacing in the harbour, we are saved!' your readers will very quickly tire of even the malicious pleasure of out-guessing your next move.

But how to ensure that your story – your ending – is *not* predictable, you ask with a bewilderment which is perfectly understandable, since we have just been discussing the inevitability which should pervade your book. It does seem at first glance as though there is no way to combine the feeling that what happens is simply the only thing that could have happened, with secretiveness and surprise, so that your readers never quite have their curiosity satisfied and are not allowed to start feeling bored and find their attention straying. In Chapter Fifteen we will examine various techniques which can be used to keep your novel simmering with interest right up to the last, inevitable paragraph on the last, inevitable page.

15
NOW YOU SEE IT, NOW YOU DON'T

THE endings of certain types of books are laid down by tradition and cannot be avoided. If you are writing a romance, your readers will expect some sort of 'happy ending' where the heroine finally surrenders (in whatever manner you choose) and true love triumphs. In a detective or crime story, the villain is at last cornered and either meets a nasty fate (which saves the author from having to detail the events of his trial, and other mundane concerns) or is removed by officers of the law.

To a certain extent, it *is* impossible to hide from your readers the events which are to come, if they know very well that the hero will win the heroine, or that the murderer will not get away. But ask yourself why readers who have read one romance, for instance, continue to read others when they too are fully aware of what the ending will be. Or why people who read crime stories would probably be extremely annoyed if the murderer, instead of meeting his Waterloo in the final chapter, daringly avoided the police trap outside Margate, boarded a convenient helicopter and made it to some remote cabin in the Canadian Rockies for a 'retirement' innocently communing with nature.

It is not the story you are telling which is, in the long run, the most enthralling aspect of your novel – it's the way you tell it. The ending is not half as important from the point of view of reader interest as the path along which you conduct them to reach that end. Hundreds of climbers can climb the same hill and reach the top – all getting to exactly the same place – but each may have a different route which they personally have discovered and prefer to follow.

Every individual passes from birth to death, from the womb to the grave, but readers never tire of a fresh slant and new illumination on these basic facts of human existence. They do not mind how many times they climb the same hill in novels, achieving practically the same – or a very similar – end, so long as the journey is one they find novel and interesting, and not a rather insipid copy of other journeys they have made before, where they can predict with bored monotony what will be around every corner.

In presenting a story where many elements may be familiar or the ending taken for granted in advance, the novelist is in something of the same position as a magician who offers his audience tricks, illusions, feats of dazzling and amazing legerdemain.

The audience at a magic show knows very well that the lady was not really cut in half, and that the gold watch which was bashed about with a sledgehammer then plunged into a bucket of water was probably not the gold watch which the chairman of the evening just handed over to the magician's glamorous assistant. It is not so dumb (it tells itself) as to fall for these slick tricks, it has all its wits about it, it can see the obvious, it's not going to be fooled by any tin-pot kids' conjurer!

Yet when confronted by the lights and the music, the roll of the drum, the breathtaking silence, the glitter of sequins and the red satin and black velvet, the sweet talk and the practiced hands of the magician, even the most hardened cases, who have 'seen it all before' and cynically refuse to accept that they are watching anything except the same old routine, will be spell-bound. It is not because the magician can really perform tricks which are superhuman and have never been done before, but because he presents them with skill, with style, with showmanship.

It's not what he actually does, in other words, it's the way that he does it which makes all the difference between a tawdry effort which will have the audience stirring restlessly in their seats, and a flawless performance.

In the same way, you must present your story with flair, use all the illusions and tricks you can to blindfold your readers to points you don't want them to notice yet, send them running enthusiastically in the wrong direction up a blind alley, hide the correct interpretation of facts from them. Subtle misdirection, false impressions planted, careful arrangement of incidents and events so that readers recall the ones you want them to recall, and forget (temporarily) about the others – all these are tools you can use to stop your story from being predictable and hold the fascinated attention of your readers.

The type of novel where this system can be seen working to the most obvious effect is a crime or detective story. Here the whole framework of the plot has to rest on misdirection, the laying of false trails, red herrings and mistaken conclusions, or else the villain would be caught in Chapter Two. But the red herrings and false trails are not there entirely for the benefit of the detective, as readers probably imagine. The successful crime novelist works out what his readers will think at any given moment in the story, anticipates their reactions and then plots some diversion which will send their thoughts careering off over the hill in quite the wrong direction.

One of the most successful tricks is to allow a traumatic event to occur – a quarrel, an accident, even an attack by intruders if you are writing this sort of book – and while the readers are absorbing the details and your characters are reacting according to their various natures, introduce another traumatic incident immediately on the heels of the first.

For instance, while your characters are sitting round drinking tea in a stunned condition, trying to recover from the fact that they have arrived home from holiday to discover their house has been thoroughly burgled, daughter Sarah arrives on the doorstep unexpectedly, in extreme distress (though what has caused the distress, whether she is involved in drug-taking, suffering from AIDS or has failed her exams at university or lost her job will of course depend on your story).

When one very significant piece of information has been brought to the attention of your readers (and the characters concerned) but you would prefer your readers did not appreciate its significance just yet, let something else happen to divert attention. As Lee and Anna are walking away from the hotel where they have found out that Joss *did* spend the night with his mysterious 'secretary', Anna can suddenly burst out that she is pregnant. Or, if this is a crime novel, Lee can catch sight of the car he has been trying to trace, disappearing out of the hotel car park, and make a mad dash after it.

I am sure you get the point. The reason why this 'double shock' can confuse readers and help you to keep them guessing, is because they can only think about a certain amount of information at a time. They might have begun to work out accurate conclusions from your first traumatic scene, begun to see the trappings behind the tinsel tricks (so to speak) and 'know' rather too much for your comfort as the writer of the novel and organiser of the whole show. When the second 'shock' happens, this will occupy all their attention and distract them from the first incident so that they forget it – for the time being.

Take advantage of this means of focusing the attention of your readers; if you want to play down any incident or fact you tell them, make sure something far more absorbing takes their mind off it immediately afterwards and diverts their interest.

Trying to conceal information from your readers, instead of using technical tricks to make them look the wrong way, will have the wrong effect. The story-teller should, within the limits of the character telling his story, always be scrupulously fair and honest with his readers. They will feel betrayed and hurt if they discover later that (for instance) Mike had known all the time that the old lady with the purple hair was his mother, because she had told him on the occasion of their first meeting in Chapter One but they had not been informed.

Any information which your characters know, which

has a bearing on the plot or development of relationships, must not be arbitrarily withheld from your readers. The novelist should not shrug, in effect, at the end and say: 'Well, yes, I did know Mike knew, but I just never got around to mentioning it – and if I had told you that, it would have spoiled my whole plot, wouldn't it?'

Beware of complications which are so immensely involved that you cannot think of any way round them except to develop wilder and wilder solutions to explain them to the reader – Mike had had an operation on his ear while he was in Canada, for example, and when the old lady with the purple hair told him she was his mother, he didn't hear her properly and thought she said 'brother'; and since she was wearing that velvet plus-fours suit, he thought she might have been his brother Jake, who was supposed to have been killed on safari but who'd maybe had a sex change...

I have been caught in this trap myself. If you find you are going to immense trouble thinking up explanations for the details in your story, and having to camouflage them at enormous expense from your readers, it is a sign that more than likely you should shelve this particular novel and start another which has a more basic, simple storyline.

It is relatively easy to set up your novel, to start with that roll of drums, let the lights dim, bring on the glamorous assistant, dazzle your readers with glitter and glamour. More difficult possibly than anything else is to sustain your presentation – sustain the strength and conviction of the way you go through your act, and never allow your novel to wilt, sag, thin out or lose its effectiveness. Tiredness, being too close to the story, lack of confidence, can all cause this.

E.M. Forster was of the opinion that 'nearly all novels go off at the end', and he also commented: 'Pity there isn't another convention, which allows a novelist to stop when he's getting out of his depth.'

Do not allow this to happen to you. Remember you are, in a certain sense, a showman. Do not let your act get out of control so that there are no more tricks, no more thrills, and your finale is just a washout. Always keep something in reserve, never write your novel constantly at the limit of your resources.

Nothing has more impact, more effectiveness in a novel than the truth. The truth about your characters, the truth about what really happened, how things really were. Try never to dodge issues, never to talk round corners, never to apologise for the story you are telling. Have the courage of your convictions. But present your act with all the showmanship and skill at your command, don't skulk about in a dark corner and hope the audience won't notice that you can't really manage some of the tricks yet.

16
THE LAST WORD

A ND SO, after weeks of effort, you are nearly there. You are
almost at the end. For the reader, the ending of a novel
appears to be final, definite, clear-cut, complete. For the
novelist, it is more likely to seem messy and bitty, requiring
careful explanation and wholesale tidying-up.

There are two main problems with endings. One is that
you should be very careful not to break off your story before
all the explanations and little technical points have been
satisfactorily dealt with and the story itself has drawn to its
natural close. The other is that many new novelists feel a
great reluctance actually to write the last word. Once you
finish your novel, you will never have any further dealings
with these characters you love, and there is sometimes a
temptation to prolong the ending until you just cannot put
the parting off any longer.

Every novel has to finish in exactly the right place, and, as
with most other sections of your book, the best way to determine where the right place should be is to consider the practical (rather than the artistic) aspect of the situation.

The last climax of a book is generally the point where your
story really ends, where the fate of your characters is decided;
but it is a mistake to finish there and just stop dead. Nearly
always, you will need to follow the big scene with a 'winding-
down' where your novel packs its bags, so to speak, before
moving on out of your reader's life.

This 'rounding-off', 'winding-down', 'tidying-up' process
might only need to occupy a few pages. In the case of a very
complicated story, however, you many require a final chapter
to deal with all the little details that have to be cleared up, the
smoothing out of queries, the disposal (often literally) of
superfluous personnel.

With regard to endings and ways in which novels resolve

119

themselves, real life is again extremely unsatisfactory if taken as a guide. The reason why so many novels allow the villain/villainess to crash the car and go up in flames while trying to escape, for instance, or fall dramatically from cliffs to their death hundreds of feet below, or even go mad in a rolling-eyed and foaming-at-the-mouth manner so that they have to be whisked off behind high walls, never to be seen again, is not because this adds to the realism of the story, rather, it's that these are useful disposal methods where the novelist can administer justice without all the inconvenience and anti-climax of questions being asked, motives being examined, extenuating circumstances being taken into account.

I must admit, I have used such short cuts myself and make no apology for doing so, as in certain types of books the author really has no alternative to making a clean sweep, as it were, of the villain or villainess without involving a great deal of tiresome minutiae which would weaken the impact of the story. Remember that what matters most is for your book to have the effect you want it to have on your readers. It is a work of art, not a documentary, so you can be quite ruthless with your characters.

If it is more effective to kill them off at the end or let them take some journey which the readers know will end in disaster, or otherwise remove them permanently from the scene, do it so long as you can think up a convincing *modus operandi*.

Shilly-shallying at the end of a book, apologetic and lame excuses, vague hints which leave the readers with the impression that the novelist couldn't be more specific because he or she didn't *know* the answers, can all weaken the whole thing and leave a very bad impression, even if the rest of the novel was good.

A symphony which ended with a few half-hearted toots would be most unlikely to continue to ring in the ears of the audience after the conductor had laid down his baton and they had departed for home. Let your novel too have its crashing chords, its moments of glory, and don't spoil them by splitting hairs and fussing afterwards. Be bold, be incisive.

Cut clean if you have to, get rid of any dead wood. There are more than enough explanations and queries that you will need to attend to without overloading your readers with information that you don't need to inflict upon them.

We have already seen that it is far better to explain as you go along, if possible, so that the book does not end with a lumpy and indigestible scene full of questions like: 'But what made you think that – ?' or 'But how on earth did you know – ?' or 'When did you first realise – ?', with appropriate replies from all the other characters, ritually filling in the full picture for the benefit of the reader.

If you do need to give a lot of explanation – in a classic type of crime novel for instance – try to make sure you do not prolong it unnecessarily, and try to keep at least one or two vital little 'twists' to enliven the scene and keep the attention of your readers. Agatha Christie's final chapters in which Hercule Poirot gathers all the protagonists together and explains who committed the crime, and how he deduced the truth, step by step, are brilliant examples of how to enthrall your readers during what might otherwise be a rather boring let-down, just a lot of dull talk when all the action is over.

Readers, nevertheless, feel cheated and indignant if things have not been settled in full before a book ends. For instance, if your heroine was puzzled early on in the story about why the hydrangeas in the garden of her new country cottage were coming up pink instead of blue, the readers will not forget this little problem, and will expect an answer somewhere along the way. A good novelist will ensure that such a trivial query is cleared up long before the inevitable round-up of explanations as the book finishes but *some* answer has to be given.

If one of your characters goes to the local library in Chapter Four for reference works on poisons or dress design or how to sing madrigals, and this is featured as part of the development of your story, the readers will, if their minds are not put at rest sooner or later, worry because there has been no mention of the library books being returned. Will the library send a card to say the books are overdue? They must be getting really annoyed by now: it's six months since

Chapter Four – will they prosecute? Or perhaps this particular library – what county is it in? – maybe they have a day when you can return overdue books without having to pay a fine?

Without your being aware of it, your readers might become far more obsessed with this particular question than with the ones you want them to worry about. Smooth their way through your novel, ease their path, do not allow for any stones they can trip over or signposts which could send them off in directions you have not made allowance for.

You have to control your readers all the way through the book, lead them in the way you want them to go. You have to make sure there is no irritating little thought unaccounted for which might get into their heads and take their minds off your beautiful story. If explanations are necessary, they must be made as briefly and clearly as possible. If questions have to be answered, make sure a satisfactory answer is at hand. And at the end, leave your readers satisfied, not only emotionally and dramatically but in a practical sense, that everything is in order, that there is nothing left to worry about and the story is finished.

THIRD INTERLUDE:
THIRD CHECK LIST

A further summing-up of points to help you with the final section of your novel, which we have examined in the last few chapters:

1. Love your characters and allow a part of your mind to become utterly and completely involved with them and their activities. If you do not love them, your readers certainly won't.

2. Keep another part of your mind detached from the emotions about which you are writing, concerned only with the mechanics of cause and effect and the technical problems of your story. Do not let either of these attitudes out weigh the other so that your novel becomes too falsely sentimental or too lacking in depth of feeling.

3. Prepare future scenes and introduce advance information so that all is in readiness for the final part of your novel and will flow smoothly.

4. Try to clear explanations and other details out of the way in small doses as you proceed, rather than letting them all pile up until the novel has reached its final climax. If there are a lot of small queries or problems still waiting to be dealt with, they will confuse and clutter the impact of your major conflict.

5. Remember that in life there are no 'endings' as such, whether happy or otherwise. Your ending is something

artificial, and must appear to grow out of the main body of the novel. Try to write with some sort of awareness in mind, right from the start, of the type of ending your book will have, even if you are not sure of exact details.

6. Let your ending seem inevitable, the only ending which was right for your book and the characters in it.

7. Avoid predictability, whereby your readers will find nothing to surprise or intrigue them in your story and will be miles ahead of you mentally.

8. Even if the ending of your story is traditional, be aware that it is the fresh and original route along which you conduct your readers to reach that end that matters. Do not give readers time to think they might have heard this story before. Dazzle them with your flair and skill, impress them with your know-how and enthusiasm. Don't be a shrinking violet so far as your writing is concerned, apologetically proffering your story for their attention as though you half-expect they will push it impatiently to one side. Raise up your curtain with a flourish of trumpets. People have written stories *like* yours, yes, but never *this* story, this altogether different and new story with your name on it. 'An original writer is not one who imitates nobody but one whom nobody can imitate', declared Francois Rene de Chateaubriand.

9. Use technique with care to gain the effects you want, to mislead, side-track or temporarily blind your readers so that you are in control of their reactions. Divert their attention if this is necessary. But never give your readers false information or withhold vital details from them.

10. Allow a 'winding-down' period, however short, after your last big scene/climax/confrontation, before ending the novel. Make sure all explanations have been made, queries answered, details attended to, and characters satisfactorily accounted for. Without snapping your book shut

rudely and abruptly in the reader's face, as it were, you can then withdraw in a decisive manner. Do not try to hang about, prolonging the final parting from your characters. Once the last line of your novel has been written and you know you have reached the end, then stop.

PART III
THE PROFESSIONAL TOUCH
PREPARATION, PRESENTATION AND SUBMISSION OF YOUR NOVEL

17
A CRITICAL EYE

So that's it, you have written a novel. You have completed it, you have typed (or written in huge capitals in red felt-tip on the last page of your manuscript) those magical words : THE END.

What now?

Some people never think beyond this point, except to imagine vaguely that their pile of typescript will in some miraculous way be commandeered by a publisher or an agent, and that within a few weeks, possibly, they will be viewing glossy copies with their name prominently displayed in bookshop windows all over the country, while envelopes containing fat royalty cheques thump through the letter-box.

A happy dream, and without it there would be a much smaller number of potential novelists. But in fact, after the whirl of euphoric bliss which will probably sweep you off your feet when you actually complete your novel comes the second stage in the process of producing your book. Your work is by no means over when the last sentence has been written. What you do after you have finished it can mark the difference between presenting a professional piece of work to publishers and producing an amateur jumble doomed to immediate failure.

Facing you after you have finished your novel is the down-to-earth task of turning your dream into a practical and saleable product you can offer to a publisher or an agent. Attention to detail here, and a refusal to be daunted by the fact that, yes, it *is* hard work, it *is* a grind, it *is* repetitive and (though you are working on your own novel) it *is* very boring, can often be more crucial and prove more important than the dramatic nights you sat up to finish Chapter Twenty and the whole day when you forgot to eat because you were so absorbed with trying to get the big climax right.

So you have reached the end. You've got your book written. What now?

When you have finished the novel, put it away and do not look at it for at least a week. The longer you leave it, the more your brain will have a chance to detach itself from the story, so that you can approach revision and editing of the manuscript with a cool head. The emotional section of your workforce will, I am afraid, have to take a back seat here.

It is highly unlikely, unless you are some sort of literary perfectionist who has written only half a page per day, and spent the following mornings polishing and revising those halves before devoting the afternoons to the next two paragraphs, that your novel will not need revision. In the course of 60,000 or 70,000 words, there will almost certainly be inconsistencies in continuity – even the author's brain cannot remember in detail everything which was written in the early pages.

Apart from making sure your story runs smoothly, check for continuity of the names you gave your characters, the spelling of those names, continuity of physical detail (remember when my heroine's eyes changed from blue to green, and nobody spotted this error?). Check that the timescales match up in the different threads of your plot – that when it is autumn in the heroine's flat, the daffodils are not merrily blooming just round the corner as the hero walks through Bloomsbury Square to his assignation with her. Check for unnecessary scenes and conversations, extra sentences you could cut out because they refer to incidents or events which you afterwards did not include, superfluous adjectives and description, pieces of narrative which slow your story down.

You may discover some parts of the story do not read clearly. Insert any small explanations which are required, clarify events or incidents that might confuse your reader. In general, tidy up and polish your novel so that it reads as clearly, as tightly and as effectively as possible. This will take time – perhaps you may need to go through the manuscript twice or even three times because there is such a lot to be done. It is true that some novelists write one draft and that is it, their book is finished, but most novelists – particularly beginners – will certainly need to revise their original copy at least once.

When I started writing novels, I wrote them by hand in spiral-bound notebooks, then typed them up, revising as I did so, into a readable typed copy. Then I revised and edited the typed copy, and in the early days typed up a second copy so that I could submit the book in a clean, clear state to a publisher. When I was able to afford it, I paid somebody else to type my second copy, as I was so sick of each book after writing it (in effect) three times, as well as spending hours on revision and editing.

Now, after a great deal of practice at writing novels, I am able to produce a first copy which, in general, needs little alteration. But though this sounds so easy, it is purely because, after years and literally hundreds of thousands of words written, I have learned from experience how to edit and revise in my head at stage one, rather than on paper at stage three. I suspect most novelists who can run off a book in one go, just like that, have learned how to do it the same way. So far as I know, nobody was ever born with a fully developed ability to edit and revise their own work instinctively as they wrote their novels. It is something that has to be learned, and the learning takes time.

It is also something which many new novelists find extremely off-putting, and not only because it is time-consuming, mundane and suspiciously like hard work. To a novelist, his novel is not just a product, a saleable commodity, one more in the pile for a publisher's reader to flip through. It is his brainchild, his baby, an extension of himself to which he has devoted hours of work and thought. It is the physical evidence of his great mental striving and effort, his literary achievement.

To a novelist, any novel he has written – particularly his first – is utterly perfect and wonderful, there has never been a novel like it. Because it represents the expenditure of a good deal of physical and mental energy, because it haunted his dreams during the agonising weeks of writing, because it is something he has lived with closely for a long period of time, the novelist will value his novel out of all proportion and will often bitterly resent criticism or suggestions that it should be altered or re-written, cut or revised.

Nearly every writer, in the first flush of euphoria at actually reaching the end of a novel, feels this way. The difference between the amateur and the professional novelist is that, once the latter has descended from the dizzy heights and cooler considerations have prevailed, when he has left the manuscript alone for a few weeks then come back to it with a critical eye, he will be able to weigh his novel up in a detached and calculating manner.

He will, if he admits to the truth, see for himself the glaring errors, the weak spots, the places where the story could be tightened or made stronger. A professional novelist sets about these tasks almost instinctively, wasting no time in self-justification or trying to cover up mistakes by, as it were, pasting over the cracks. A certain amount of milk has to be spilt in the sheer wordage and volume of thinking that makes up a novel. If your book is worth anything, it is worth the expenditure of the time and energy necessary to edit it as effectively as you can, to polish it to the best of your ability so it will shine like a beautiful jewel.

You may be unable to see any error at all in your novel and consider that I quite obviously have never come across Real Art or else I would not harp on in this tiresome manner when, after all, you are an author; what are editors for if not to do the editing? You will find, however, that most publishers you are likely to encounter hold the same regrettably low and commercial views as myself when it comes to having a professional attitude to novel-writing. Even High Art is often better for a little re-working. Dylan Thomas and Proust wrote their great works in pencil on scraps of paper; but if you presented yours in this state, the only reputation you would carve out for yourself would not be one you would enjoy.

Artistically temperamented or otherwise sensitive souls sometimes feel that *their* novel is exempt from the little disciplines which the rest of us novelists have to accept. But it is professional and polite to present a good, clear and readable manuscript which is a finished job, rather than some sort of jumble which you hope vaguely that an editor will be able to translate into the masterpiece it really is. Your novel, in its original first draft, remains only half-written until you have taken the trouble to go through and do your revision and editing.

You may feel you do not have much idea about how to edit. Possibly not, but use your common sense, follow the rules which have been laid down in this book on clarity of thought, avoid clutter and side-tracking, try to keep the lines of your book as clear as possible, and most of all, be aware of what you wanted to say, how you tried to obtain your effects, and whether you think you succeeded. More than that you cannot do, and nobody would expect you to. In fact, if you have done a good job on all these points, that is probably better than the average novelist, so do what you reasonably can and then leave it.

Avoid the state similar to that of the writer we met earlier in the book, who was always sending off for background material and researching his novel, but who never actually wrote it. After completing your novel, it is very tempting to feel so proud of yourself for achieving this remarkable feat – and so easy, comparatively, to sit in an easy chair with a cup of coffee and the manuscript on your knee, pottering through it, happily jotting down a small alteration here – a more appropriate word there – that this 'editing' and 'revision' can turn into a way of life. The hard graft is done. You have actual evidence that you have written a novel. Nobody can argue with you.

Do not spend your declining years eternally tinkering with your novel, never quite getting it right, carrying the manuscript round to meetings and reading bits aloud to your admirers, waving letters from publishers who have expressed interest and who can't wait to read it – but never actually submitting it to the commercial jungle and therefore never risking rejection and the fact that it may not make the grade.

Only the cowardly choose a life of complacent self-admiration based on the fact that they have actually written a novel and reached the end. As we have seen, this is where the story *really* starts.

18
HOW TO BE
UN-PUT-DOWN-ABLE

IT is every novelist's dream to be able to produce a book which keeps readers up until three in the morning and has them glued to the story so hard they forget to leave the bus at the right stop, or miss their plane because they were so enthralled they didn't hear the boarding call. Nobody has ever been able to define the special ingredient which novels of this quality possess. They are not always great literature, and the most usual way of referring to them is to say they are 'good story-telling'.

If you can bring this quality to your novel, you will stand miles ahead in the queue so far as publishers are concerned. Some firms call it 'un-put-down-ability' and state quite frankly that it is something they are always on the lookout for in a new author. Even if your book is not suitable for them, they will take an interest and remember you if they think you have the 'magic touch' that can keep readers reading.

So how does one imbue a story with this irresistible magic, and why have I mentioned it here rather than in the section dealing with the actual writing of your novel?

Most writers assume that the ability to be 'un-put-down-able' is a secret skill that has to be mastered before one tackles the writing of one's book, and which can then be used to make the text eye-grabbing and reader-proof. It is generally considered by beginners that successful novelists would probably not be so successful without this magical ingredient, which they have obviously been endowed with in the same way as the rich are born with silver spoons in their mouths. Successful novelists, it is widely thought, were born successful, they never had to scrape and slave and struggle in penniless anonymity – and all because they were blessed with this priceless gift of being able to produce 'un-put-down-able' prose!

In fact, it is not a gift at all. Neither is it the product of some secret formula, to be scattered across each page as your book is written, nor a skill which will enable you to write in such a way that every sentence 'naturally' comes from your pen perfect, and you don't have to work at your writing.

'Un-put-down-ability' is not a gloss which those in the know can slick over their novel; it is not some special ability to be able to create unforgettable plots or particularly endearing characters. It is a state of mind, a willingness to undertake not only the basic editing and revision of your novel, but to go far beyond superficial tidying up and spend time pulling every thread of your book as taut and clear as possible. As with a lot of 'magic formulae', the truth about 'un-put-down-ability' is dismayingly prosaic and once again sounds like hard work instead of something exciting and glamorous.

In spite of what a lot of people imagine, there is in fact, very little that is glamorous about writing a novel, and a great deal that spells out hard work. Like 'un-put-down-ability'.

We have already seen that awareness of cause and effect, of the mechanics of how a novel is crafted and put together, will assist you in producing the effects you want and enable you to control the responses and reactions of your readers. 'Un-put-down-ability' is at this stage no more and no less than a minute attention to the clarity of your story, the logical progression from beginning to end, the cutting out of anything that might clutter it, distract your readers, or allow them a moment when they feel they can catch their breath.

Once a reader feels there is a lull in the story, a slightly less interesting scene, a moment when the author allowed the text to ramble a bit, he will look up from the page and stretch, make a cup of coffee, decide he had better take the dog for a walk or do whatever else needs to be done. He will put the book down. Later, he will pick it up and carry on with the next chapter, but for the moment, the novelist has lost him.

Aim, when revising your novel and correcting your manuscript, to achieve such clear-cut exposition of your story, such tight writing with no superfluous words, sentences, details, descriptions, explanations or whatever that there will be *no single moment* when the reader will feel the pressure is off, the novelist is looking the other way, he's free to escape for a few seconds and get off that bus or catch that plane. In other words, let there be no single slip-shod, careless, vague, woolly, less-than-your-best word or thought in your book.

Even if you feel you lack the skills of a professional editor, publishers will appreciate that you have done a good job at presenting your manuscript in as clear and well-put-together a manner as you can. The fact that you took the trouble to think about every smallest detail, too, will not escape their notice. A professional – in my experience as a novelist, at any rate – is the writer who never tries to shirk the boring parts of a job, the revision, the editing, the second and third drafting. Only second-rate beginners who will never make the grade think they will get away with a half-finished effort because they have done the bit they enjoyed and the rest seems like work.

Do not try to console yourself with the fact that 'nobody will notice' that awkward scene in Chapter Three, or assume that the book is so long that the conversations you know need rewriting will be skipped over anyway so you need not bother. Like 'un-put-down-ability', professionalism too is an attitude of mind, and one that publishers will be quick to recognise.

19
IN MANUSCRIPT

THE final copy of your novel, when every last word of revision, alteration and polishing has been done, is the one that will be read by publishers, editors and agents. It should be free from corrections and additions, if possible, and should exist as something which is basically clear and can be handled easily – several people will have to read it even while it is being considered at one publishing house.

There are few strict rules about how you should present your novel. Nowadays, a hand-written manuscript will immediately damn your work as amateurish and therefore unlikely to stand up in today's highly competitive market. Do not submit your work hand-written. Not only will it look amateurish, but it's a brave editor or reader who is prepared in these days of stress and eye-strain to plough through a hand-written novel, and you will be giving your book no chance of making a good first impression.

The most convenient size of paper to use for your final copy is A4, and you should set your work out on one side only of each page, in double-spacing, with margins of at least one inch on both sides, not just on the left. Publishers do not make these rules out of sheer awkwardness, which is what a lot of beginner writers think.

Editors will be frustrated as they are working on your book, if there are no margins where they can mark their alterations and instructions to the printers. So leave plenty of space. Those short-sighted publishers with eye-strain will appreciate the fact that your novel is in double-spacing, too and when your book is accepted and sent to the typesetters for the text to be set, they will work from copy on one side of the page only.

It is wise to start each section, each part and each chapter, on a separate page and mark it clearly. Most vital for a novel, though, is that you should number the pages throughout the novel, consecutively and never by chapter. You could add an identifying word at the top of each page to your number. If you were submitting *Concrete* in manuscript, you could use the title so that the pages read: *concrete – 1, concrete – 2, concrete – 3* and so on. If your book was called *It's What's Left When The Clothes Are Off That Makes The Man*, use the tag-word 'man', so that your pages read: *man – 1, man – 2, man – 3*.

The reason for this is in case, as has been known to happen, an editor or publisher who is reading your manuscript and has several other manuscripts piled up next to his cup of coffee, overflowing ashtray, bottle of headache pills and lotion for sore eyes, might inadvertently knock the pile so that all those pages scatter on the floor. If each manuscript of several hundred sheets has only been marked with a number at the top of the page, it could take the poor overworked editor quite a long time to figure out, after he has picked up the pages, which ones belong with which novel, so some sort of identification can be of immense assistance.

I have even known cases where manuscripts were accidentally split into half, and a title-less and unidentifiable second part of a novel sat about waiting for someone to claim it. In fairness, horror stories about lost manuscripts, damaged manuscripts, manuscripts that publishers left on the Underground when they got off at Goodge Street, or which the family dog chomped into shreds when it was being read over the weekend at home, are largely exaggerated. Most publishers, agents and anyone else to whom you might submit your novel will take great care of everything they receive and do their utmost to ensure that if it has to be returned to you, it will arrive in the same state as you despatched it.

The completed manuscript – the length of which you calculate from the number of words per page, and the number of pages in the book, in the manner we have already discussed – will probably run to several hundred pages, possibly five or six hundred. You may feel it is a good idea to bind them in some way to keep them together, before you submit them to a publisher. In general, however, the best and most helpful thing to do is to leave them loose and submit them either in an envelope-style folder which will take them all comfortably, or else in a box – possibly the box which contained the paper you used when typing up or printing out your novel.

Any sort of binder makes a manuscript difficult to read. The paper tears as the reader tries to flatten pages in order to see what the first word on each line is; or else the whole lot falls out of the binder when he tries to loosen its strangling grasp, and will not go in again, so that he ends up cursing beneath his breath at the paper, the binder, the novel and you the author. Under these circumstances, he will not feel inclined to be well-disposed towards your book even if he eventually succeeds in reading it. Loose pages are much easier to cope with, especially with an identifying word at the top of every page, just in case of an accident.

Apart from the actual text of your book, what else should you include as part of your manuscript? You will need a title page, upon which should be typed the title of your novel, the author's name – your own if you intend to write under your own name, your pseudonym if you have one – and also your name, address and telephone number. Some authorities insist that the length of the manuscript should be included, so if you have calculated this, add it.

Pseudonyms cause many new writers quite a lot of concern. There is nothing legal or complicated about them. Anyone can write a book and publish it under a name which is not legally his – so long as he is not using the name of a real and recognisable person, or trying to infer that his book was written by someone else, or otherwise attempting to mislead the public. You do not have to register a pseudonym, copyright it or take any legal action about it. Simply put it on your title page as the name of the author of your novel. When you receive a contract from your publisher it will be clearly stated that, though the publisher is making an agreement with Hermione

Twistlewise, the author, her novel will be appearing in published form as *Concrete* by Jess-Ann Argent (your pseudonym).

Even if you want to lurk, hermit-like, in the background and keep your writing a deadly secret, it is essential that you include your real name, as author, with your address and telephone number when you send your novel to a publisher. He will want to know just who he is dealing with, and will not take kindly to coyness about 'preferring my employees do not know that I write romantic stories, so I have sent them to you under the name of our post-mistress, who reads a lot of your books'.

A publisher (or agent) will not care in the least that, though you may be a burly seventeen-stone lorry-driver, you want your tender love stories published under the name of Dawn Rose. Relatives and people you know might be gossipy, but publishers can keep a secret. If you do not want your real identity made public, they will not give you away.

Apart from a title page, you may need to include any other information you want to give readers, in the form of an Author's Note. Comments about whether the story is based on fact, information about the locations you have used, and changes you have made in them for the purpose of the story, mention of references you have consulted and people who have been particularly helpful could usefully be given here, though you may prefer to include a list of factual sources separately, if it is a long one. Some writers also put in a special Acknowledgements note, thanking the people who have assisted during the writing of the book. It is up to you how you choose to word these if you feel you want to include them.

Acknowledgement must be made of copyright material used, if any, and a separate book on copyright is to be published in this series.

It used to be very common for chapters in a novel to have titles, which were of course listed on the contents page. If you really want to give each of your chapters a title, by all means do so, and include a contents page after your title sheet, with the chapters and their titles listed. Note, though, that the trend now is for untitled chapters, and when we consider what sort of titles used to be inflicted on readers, the reason for their demise is obvious.

From a romantic novel of the thirties, sample chapter titles are : *Reggie Shows the White Feather*; *'To Love is to Suffer'*; *A Shock for Dolly!*; *'He Will Never Get You!'* Chapter titles in a novel are generally superfluous and will give your work an old-fashioned air. As we have already seen, the readers who will be reading your book are altogether a different breed from readers of the past. They don't have to have everything spelled out for them. They like to make up their own minds, and you can't win your way into their hearts by dangling the promise of delights to come before them in juicy chapter headings. They are too sophisticated and too literate for that.

Whatever else you might or might not feel you need to include in these opening notes, lists, titles and so on – which we call the 'prelims' or preliminary pages before the actual text of your story starts – it is almost certain that the item which will give you the most pleasure to complete – the finishing touch you can award yourself as a treat when everything else is done and the final copy is almost ready to submit to a publisher – will be the line where you record the dedication of your great work. It may take you days, even weeks, to decide on your dedicatee(s) and to compose the sentence of dedication to your own satisfaction. Savour it to the full, as bestowing a dedication is one of the real pleasures a novelist can feel free to enjoy with a clear conscience, when the hard work and toil is all but over.

It is a good idea to make sure any preliminary pages you include are all marked at the top with your identifying word, ie *concrete – dedication*; *concrete – author's note.* The only one which does not need this as a tag-word is the title page, which already has the title marked on it clearly. Do not try to cram every note you are including, lists, acknowledgements, dedication and all, onto the same page even though they might only be one or two sentences in length. Put them on separate sheets with their identifying word, and the heading you want them to have, or else no heading at all. Each page will be marked by your editor with instructions for the typesetter, and the fact that everything is on separate sheets will make this easier and clearer for all concerned.

It makes no difference whether your novel appears in its final form typewritten on a manual, electric or electronic machine, or printed on a word processor, so long as the print is clear and readable. As I write, there is some discrimination against dot-matrix, but this does not mean you should panic because your own machine prints dot-matrix and rush out to buy another. My own machine prints dot-matrix; it is clear and readable and has caused me no problems. Clarity, and a recollection of those short-sighted publishers whose way has to be made easy, should dictate the rules if questions arise here, but obviously you would be unwise to submit a manuscript which looks like somebody's bank statement, on one eternal page of print-out paper folded like a giant concertina.

Do not try to be clever and original when you set out your text. Publishers will not be impressed. They prefer manuscripts which are simply and clearly laid out in a traditional manner. If you want to indicate a break in the text, you can leave four spaces between lines instead of just double-spacing. Avoid multitudes of asterisks. They irritate publishers. If you must use some mark to indicate a break in your text, just one asterisk(*) will do.

Whatever physical form your final draft takes, whether typed up, printed out or stored on a disc, it is vital that you always have a copy of the text yourself and *never* let your only carbon or disc out of your possession, even if it is to a publisher who swears it will be in production tomorrow or a film company which is talking about a million-dollar option. They may well mean every word, but if they have the only copy of your novel and they happen to mislay it, or it gets lost in transit, you would be in a very awkward situation indeed.

I have even read hints on writing in the past, where it

has been suggested you should let a friend keep a spare copy of your manuscript in case your house catches fire and your own copy (and all that hard work) goes up in flames. One could become obsessed about this, worrying about the danger of fire in your friend's home as well, so why not send a third copy to Aunt Flo in Wapping, just in case?

Here there is yet another of the little backwaters we have seen waiting for unwary writers, along with the fate of the researcher-who-never-wrote and the revision-mad-perfectionist who is still 'working on' his manuscript fifty years later. We could so easily become very conscious of the possible danger of fire, flood, leaking water-tanks and pipes, spontaneous combustion, radiation and so forth, and spend all our time making copies of the few pages we actually managed to complete, in order to ensure that they could be distributed to as many different locales as possible where fire/crime/suicide rates were low, in an attempt to ensure that at least one copy would survive.

Without going to these extremes, try to cover yourself against accidents to your manuscript so far as you reasonably can. It would be a terrible thing to happen to the author of any novel if, as he was pressing manfully on with his last few pages, his only copy of the first three hundred was, by whatever means, destroyed. Writers have been known to re-write novels if the original has disappeared – I have mentioned that I have done it myself – but it is a thankless task and enough to break an author's heart, especially if the novel was a first effort.

Make sure, within reason, that there is always a copy of your book safe somewhere, just in case.

20
PUBLISHER OR AGENT?

WITH the whole of your novel in the can and an impressively clear and readable copy waiting to be sent off to meet its fate, the time comes to consider, if you have not done so already, the best place to submit your book.

In the days before agents existed in such profusion, a novelist would automatically have contacted a publisher, in the hope that the publisher would like his novel and would agree to publish it. Now, a lot of people feel that an agent is a sort of alternative, that if they can unload their novel onto an agent, it is practically the same thing as signing a publisher's contract.

In fact, it is not. At best, an agent provides you with a half-way stopover, a friendly word of encouragement and the knowledge that, well, one other person beside yourself likes the book. But the agent still has to interest a publisher in your work before you are able to celebrate the signing of your contract and the fact that your novel has been sold.

If you are a new writer and this is your first novel, or even if you have had some modest success with articles and stories, maybe written two or three novels but have not managed to place any of them so far, you will probably find that it is difficult to persuade an agent to take you on his books as a client. Unfair though it may be, agents like to see evidence that the writers they represent have good track records. They are reluctant to handle the work of untried and new novelists unless it is obvious at a glance that the novel is something very special which has real potential to create publishing history.

The reason for this is that agents are in the business to make a living. As middlemen between author and publisher, their income derives from the percentage they take on the sale of their clients' work. They are not unnaturally dubious about handling the work of beginners who may, in spite of a certain amount of promise, never actually get into print at all.

Also, new writers are an unknown quantity so far as future work is concerned. An agent likes his clients to keep producing material he can sell. A beginner with no books to his credit might have written an interesting first novel, but has the agent any guarantee he will write another?

It is generally recognised that there is a vicious circle at work when trying to get agents to handle your work. If you have no professionally published material, they are not interested; therefore it is difficult to get your books published since you cannot submit them through an agent; therefore you do not get them published; therefore no agent is interested.

However, all is not lost. If you do want to try and get your book handled by an agent, then the best of luck! If you succeed and your agent is a reputable one, little more needs to be said. Your troubles could well be over since your agent will do his best to sell your book advantageously, and will handle all aspects of the sale on your behalf, plus any other sales of subsidiary rights that might arise.

If, on the other hand, you cannot interest an agent and are forced to fall back on your own resources or if you decide to deal directly with a publisher yourself right from the start – you are not condemned to some sort of inferior 'tradesman's entrance' when it comes to submitting your own work. By and large, you stand just as much of a chance of success.

Nearly all publishers who publish fiction are willing to read the novels submitted to them, whether these are by established authors, sent in by agents, or come from strangers they have never heard of. They are constantly interested in new novels because they keep hoping that, sooner or later, they will strike gold in the form of a brilliant first book that will fall into their lap, or an author who has written *the* novel of the decade and is certain to scoop all the literary prizes.

If you ask a publisher: 'What sort of thing are you looking for?' he will probably (unless he deals in 'formula' books) be unable to tell you. He doesn't know what he is looking for in a novel, he only knows that he will know it when he sees it. And so everything which is submitted to his office will be read, however cursorily.

Many embittered would-be writers claim that their novel was returned without having been read. Some even try to trap the publisher's reader by glueing page 121 to page 122 and page 549 to 550, and inspecting these pages on the return of the manuscript to see whether they have been pulled apart or (as they usually discover) whether they are still glued together. This proves the manuscript was not read, they claim.

In fact, it proves not that publishers do not read the work submitted to them, but that an experienced reader was able to tell from the first few pages, or perhaps from the first few chapters and then a quick dip into the text towards the end, that this fell well below anything like publishable standard and was in fact hopeless.

So what are the rules when submitting your novel to a publisher for his consideration?

First, be reasonably certain that the publisher you choose does in fact publish fiction, and fiction of the same type as your own book. You can examine the sort of books different publishers publish by browsing in the library or a few bookshops. Details of publishers' requirements can be obtained from the various writers' handbooks* which you can also consult in a library, if you do not possess your own copies. Publishers' catalogues give details of their latest publications, and can be obtained from their offices on the expenditure of a polite request and a stamped addressed envelope.

Some publishers are even more helpful to authors and issue their own Guidelines to assist new writers. Details of

The Writers' & Artists' Yearbook (A & C Black) and *The Writer's Handbook* (Macmillan) appear in up-to-date editions annually.

preferred lengths, topics which are taboo, whether they have a preference for first or third person narratives, what sort of readership they aim their books at, whether explicit sex is permitted, and so on, are often available if you write and ask for information.

I need hardly point out that it would be more useful to write your novel, *after* investigating as many requirements of publishers as possible, but it is a fact of life in the writing world that most people who decide to write a novel complete it before they even start to consider the commercial angles of book publishing.

Try to submit your novel to a publisher who will treat it seriously because it is the sort of novel he habitually handles, rather than one who will send it back by the next post because he does not deal with romance/crime/westerns/anything less than 100,000 words in length/anything over 45,000 words in length/ghost stories/humour or whatever. So far as possible, try to ensure your book falls within his requirements of length and style – popular library story as opposed to erudite intellectual exercise, for example, or violent Third World statement as opposed to stylish English horror classic.

Do not, in other words, submit your violent Third World statement novel to a publisher whose main concern is formula romance. Never kid yourself that if it is good, he will change his publishing policy in order to accommodate it. The most you might get would be a mention of some suitable firm to whom you could submit it when it was returned. More than likely, however, it would come back with a rejection slip and a silent curse from the publisher because you were not professional enough to investigate the sort of novels he publishes, and so wasted his office staff's valuable time with a completely unsuitable submission.

What do you send with your manuscript? Apart from making sure that your name, address and telephone number are prominently printed on the box or file containing your novel, as well as on the title page, the only vital item you need enclose is a stamped self-addressed envelope* or label for the return of the manuscript if this should be necessary. Publishers are generally courteous to everyone, even unknown new authors, but this does not run to paying heavy postage bills on hundreds of pages of manuscript which are quite unsuitable for publication, and which they did not even ask to see.

As a novelist you are in business just as surely as the publisher, so keep the machinery running smoothly whenever you send out your manuscript and cover return postage just in case. Otherwise you can blame nobody but yourself if you find after a year that the manuscript has been sitting about with other rejected manuscripts in the corner of somebody's office, all waiting for return postage to be paid on them, since none was enclosed. Publishers do not want to keep manuscripts for which they have no use, but they are not charity concerns.

Should you send your novel to more than one publisher at the same time? This is always frowned upon and it is never a wise or sensible thing to do. In order to by-pass the problem – and to speed up the lengthy process of submission and consideration, with possible delays as the manuscript is read by several different readers and editors, and a wait of anything up to six months or a year before you even know whether it has been rejected – some authorities suggest an initial approach by letter to selected publishers, with a brief description of your novel and any relevant details such as the length and a summary of the plot. A few sample pages to illustrate your style of writing might usefully be included.

It is generally felt that this way you will, without being unethical and submitting your novel to several different publishers at once, be able to make your first serious submission to a publisher who has responded favourably to your clutch of letters and shown an interest in your work. If several publishers have asked to see the manuscript you can make a list and submit them in turn,

If you live outside the UK or want to send your novel abroad, do not send stamps. International Reply Coupons to cover the cost of the postage can be obtained from Post Offices if you ask for them.

putting the most likely names high on the list and the least likely towards the end.

In addition to being able to make your first submission to a firm where you would appear to stand more of a chance of success than if you just sent off your manuscript at random, it is argued, you will have the names of the editors or editorial staff who signed the letters asking to see your work, to whom to address your parcel. This, surely, can't be bad!

My own feeling here, though, is that any advantage you will gain from this performance is largely psychological. It might well seem rather exciting to be receiving letters from publishing houses, with publishers' logos and names on the envelopes, and to be able to show friends actual evidence that the publishers in question are willing to consider your manuscript if you would like to send it along. They must be interested, they must think it sounds good. You may even feel that with all this encouragement, it is only a matter of wrapping the manuscript up, just a question of time.

The truth is that, as we have seen, publishers are so determined not to miss the great new novel of the era or the blooming of a wonderfully prolific talent which might bring paperback royalties pouring in for the next fifty years, that unless your outline and sample pages struck them as highly unlikely ever to bear any resemblance to anything remotely resembling good literature, they will generally agree optimistically to read any book which sounds as if it might be vaguely interesting. This does not necessarily mean they think they will want to accept it; it means they want to have a look just to make sure no unsuspected nugget is slipping through in the eternal panning for literary gold.

So if you have chosen your publisher carefully before you make your submission, you stand as much of a chance, generally, if you send the completed manuscript straight off in the first place. As for knowing the name of the right editor to whom to address your manuscript, this makes little difference as most publishing houses have their own system through which all unsolicited work is passed. It is not until a novel has been read by one or two outside readers, usually, that an editor becomes involved, so even if you marked the name of Camilla Harton-Dyffryn (who invited you to send your book along) all over your parcel, it would probably still go with the rest of the mail to Ginny and Cheri in the Downstairs Office.

Enclose your manuscript with a stamped self-addressed envelope or label, and add a brief covering letter, informing the publisher that you are submitting your novel *Concrete* by Jess-Ann Argent for his consideration. Do not write several pages explaining how you always had an ambition to be a writer, but though you won all the literary prizes at school and everyone has always said you really ought to write a book, you have never actually been able to settle down to a novel until now, when the boys are at university and your husband/wife has retired and you both have a lot more time, etc, etc.

All the publisher's reader is concerned about is what lies between the title page and the last paragraph of your novel, and whether it is good. If it is, and the publisher wants to hear more about you, he will let you know. Otherwise, keep your life history to yourself.

Send your novel off and if possible forget about it. You are unlikely to hear anything for at least a few weeks, and though some publishers may be able to give you a decision within six weeks or two months, others take longer. If you have heard nothing after six weeks, you could reasonably write a polite enquiry as to whether a decision has yet been reached about your novel *Concrete* by Jess-Ann Argent. If you have heard nothing after a further month, say, it would be in order to phone up and ask whether there is any delay about your novel. You will probably find in all cases that the editorial staff will be helpful and anxious to put you in the picture about what might be happening.

All sorts of things can cause delay – readers may have just gone on holiday, staff may have just gone on holiday, someone could be ill and away from the office. More excitingly, your novel may have been given a favourable report by the first reader and might now be with a second. Or the second, too, might have been impressed and the typescript currently be with Camilla Harton-Dyffryn, the fiction editor. Even this is not the end, as your novel will have to run the gauntlet of editorial conferences, planning, sales and marketing meetings, before you actually get a letter offering to publish *Concrete* and outlining the terms the publisher hopes you will find acceptable.

But what if, somewhere along the line, the 'thumbs down' is given, and instead of that wonderful thin letter of acceptance, the all-too-familiar bulky parcel comes back? Even worse, what if it comes back from the second publisher you send it to? And the third?

This game is not for the cowardly, as we have already seen. If you can't stand the heat, keep out of the kitchen. If you do not possess the necessary determination, perseverance, confidence that what you are doing is worthwhile – sheer guts, in fact – then join the ranks of those faint-hearted souls who are still 'researching my novel' or (with a very unconvincing display of modesty) being urged to give a reading of their typescript – 'as yet only a rough copy, you understand, I have a lot of revision still to do' – before an admiring audience at the village hall.

Make a list of suitable publishers, either from the reactions you get to letters you send out or from your own research into what the different publishers seem to be publishing. If your book comes back from the first name on the list, remove any evidence that it has been away before, tidy it up so it looks fresh, then send it to number two. Then (if necessary) to number three. And number four.

And what do you do meanwhile, since it could take a long time – several years maybe – before you get down the list to number six? Well, if you are the writer I think you are, you will have got your novel as finished and as polished as you possibly can, packed it off to the first publisher you think might be interested in it, and then, instead of sitting about biting your nails and worrying, you will have begun to get stuck into – your *next* book.

PART IV
THE GENRE NOVEL

21
THE SAME OLD STORY

GENRE novels are books which can be fitted into categories and which have to be written to certain rules in order to meet the publishers' requirements. By and large, they are constructed to formulae and follow patterns which do not vary much from book to book. As we have seen, readers of romance, say, or westerns, will expect certain ingredients to be included in the story and will not welcome unpredictability or a radical 'new' slant on the subject; they would not appreciate a romance being told from the point of view of the heroine's elderly aunt, for instance, or a western narrated in equine fashion by the hero's trusty palomino!

Publishers who deal with category or genre books can usually be identified with little difficulty if you consult the writers' handbooks or, as when dealing with general fiction, examine the types of novels that are available in libraries and bookshops.

If you decide you would like to undertake some specialised sort of novel, make sure you have studied the genre and are familiar with its rules, both obvious, such as the viewpoint from which the story is usually told, and others implicit and hinted at, which may not be so easily identified. In general, you would be wise not to attempt any type of 'formula' novel unless you have at least a certain amount of sympathy and appreciation for this sort of story.

There have been celebrated cases of hardened ex-servicemen churning out successful romance, however, and some of the most popular crime novelists writing today are women, so there are no barriers so long as you can produce what the publishers are looking for. In addition, there is a greater turnover of category and 'formula'

155

novels because of their huge guaranteed readership, so you will stand a better chance of being able to place a book specially tailored to the romance or the saga or the fantasy market.

The main thing here is to be sure you know exactly what is required. Many publishers are only too willing to provide new authors with guidelines and if you are attempting a formula novel, you could well find that the publishers will be prepared to work with you and give you editorial help and guidance along the way.

For a formula novel, you can submit the first two or three chapters along with a synopsis of the rest of the plot, and publishers will usually accept these for consideration. This way, you do not need to complete the whole book before you ask for a publisher's opinion on it. If he thinks you show promise, he will perhaps suggest ways in which your plot-line can be improved, or one of his editors might approve the book chapter by chapter as you write it, and advise on the best ways to make the whole thing work. You might even be invited to the office for a general discussion.

Because genre books follow certain formulae, they are usually the work of skilled professionals rather than new writers – though many new novelists have their first success in romance or crime. There is a constant demand for skilled writers to fill in any gaps that might be left (for whatever reason) in the ranks of romance or crime novelists. This is why publishers are so willing to offer help and encouragement to new blood. Writers with skill and experience are going to be needed to keep the presses rolling with the genre novels of tomorrow.

22
THE ROMANTIC
NOVEL

A romantic novel, whether or not it incorporates some sort of sub-plot about a business takeover or an attempt to set up a holiday colony in a hitherto unspoiled part of the heroine's beloved Cornwall, is basically the story of two people – the heroine and the hero – and how they meet, overcome obstacles in the way of their realisation that they love each other, and finally succumb to their mutual and eternal passion and devotion.

The heroine is the main character in a romance – except in rare cases which are not typical – and the story should be told through her eyes. Next most important is the hero. The formula dictates that he must appear in the early pages of the novel. A 'love at first sight' meeting near the end of the book and a whirlwind wedding after three days is just not on.

You can work the formula so that the heroine marries in the early pages of a romance, sometimes without knowing much about the man she weds; but then the story must concern itself with all the misunderstandings that have to work themselves out after the wedding, before the heroine realises she really respects and loves him.

It is a rule in romance that – again except in certain unusual cases – the heroine has to be a virgin, even if this is not directly stated. She may perhaps have had some sexual experience in the past, with a character who reappears, much to her chagrin, in the early pages of the book, making her squirm at the memory of her previous encounters with him, but it will be quite obvious to knowledgeable romance-goers that this obnoxious type is of course the hero, whom she will eventually realise she loves.

Quite explicit sexual scenes are now permitted in romances, where only a few years back, the hero and the heroine could never progress further than a passionate embrace and a row of asterisks. The heroine, however, is never allowed to have sexual relations with anyone other than the man she is, in the end, going to love (and since all romantic heroes always see the light at last, however much they have played around with women in the past – the man she is going to marry!)

It can be possible for the hero to have had quite a lot of sexual experience; he must generally be presented as a man of the world. Sometimes the heroine may be a widow who has to overcome her memories of her dead husband, but the reader must always have it made clear to him or her that only when the heroine has finally met her hero in this book will sexual attraction be truly wonderful and meaningful. It will denote the coming together of souls as well as bodies, too, since what hero and heroine are now experiencing is True Love, something neither of them really knew in the past before.

THE HEROINE

Until fairly recently – and sometimes straying into romances written even now – heroines had to be completely beautiful, with nothing to mar the delicate oval face, the widely spaced eyes (often of some improbable colour like violet), the perfectly shaped nose and tender mouth. They were also the possessors of perfect figures.

Now, thankfully, the trend is for more human heroines with endearing blots on their perfection, such as a tip-tilted nose, a too-wide mouth (this is very popular, since it hints at unsuspected depths of passion), or even slightly crooked teeth. Freckles have also come into their own, but your heroine should always be on the slender side – no romantic heroines are ever fat, or even tubby! Long hair is popular, although you can get away with short hair; and your heroine may be either very petite or tall – but the hero must always be taller than she is, even if she is six feet.

Your heroine ought to be aged about 18 to 24. Occasionally there are heroines of up to 29, but these are rare cases. The most popular age is 19 to 21. She must be a creature of spirit and independence and perhaps have a penchant for doing good turns or an endearingly scatter-brained nature. She might on the other hand be so infuriatingly efficient that the reader will enjoy seeing the hero bring her down.

Let her have a sense of humour and be able to see the funny side of even her worst moments. And all heroines are invariably honest with themselves, even if they try hard to cover up their real feelings from other people. Your heroine should not be too intellectual, or too far removed from the humdrum ticking-over of everyday life as the general public sees it. Even if she is a rich girl or somebody who lives an extremely sheltered life, she will have a maid, or more likely a friend, who is wise-cracking and realistic and has her feet firmly on the ground.

THE HERO

As has been mentioned, the hero needs to make his appearance very early on in the book. He may be someone the heroine knew as a young girl, or somebody with whom she once had a disastrous encounter and whom she longs to forget (or thinks she does). It is a common occurrence in a romance for the heroine to take an immediate dislike to the hero, and carry on quivering with wrath and spitting with outrage every time she sees him, until in the last paragraph she realises she has really loved him all along.

This is to over-simplify; but remember that love and hate can run side by side. Let your hero and your heroine feel some strong emotion at their first encounter. It may not be recognisable as love, but if they react very strongly to each other, and continue to do so, the readers will find it perfectly acceptable that they should, as they come to know and respect each other better, revise their opinions without realising it until they see that what they feel is love.

The hero of today is generally an 'older man' – in his early or mid-thirties at the very least, and proportionately older according to the age of the heroine. He should be roughly fifteen years older than she is. He is always a striking personality. He may be handsome, but more usually he has something more than just good looks, which draws the attention of every woman he meets. He is inclined to an almost animal sexuality, and is often built like an all-in wrestler – particularly if he happens to be something with out-of-door connections, like a forestry expert.

Heroes are never newsagents, butchers or policemen. They are never serving apprenticeships or working for exams. They are usually rich, and are generally as high as it is possible to climb in their profession – they own fast cars, silk shirts and hand-made Italian shoes. Or alternatively, they have a title and a crumbling castle in Scotland, but spend their time pottering round the estate in thigh-hugging jeans and sweatshirts, trying to work out ways to raise money to repair the roof and stop it leaking.

The hero may be autocratic, moody, downright rude, but you must never allow him to be unjust, petty or deliberately dishonest. He must win and retain the respect – and eventually, the love – of the heroine. We have to believe that he will, once she has surrendered herself to him, love, honour and protect her effectively.

You may give your hero moments of weakness, but make sure they are for reasons the heroine and the reader can accept. Heroes never get sinus trouble, for instance, or nosebleeds; they never have ingrowing toenails or impacted wisdom teeth. They can have flu, or even a touch of something rather exotic like malaria if they have travelled abroad, since this is relatively dignified and also allows the heroine to nurse the delirious patient.

SUPPORTING CHARACTERS

Depending on the story, the supporting cast in a romance usually contains either an 'other woman' or an 'other man' or both. The 'other woman' generally appears about halfway through, out of the hero's past, and is often a model or a previous girlfriend. Nearly always, she is beautiful, rich and proprietorial towards the hero, and her heroine feels she will never be able to compete with such sophistication.

The 'other man' is generally a former friend or boyfriend of the heroine, or some sympathetic admirer to whom she turns when she feels she can't stand that odious hero-type for another minute and needs a boost to her confidence. Usually these characters are useful to the author either as foils for highlighting the sterling qualities of the hero to the heroine and vice versa, or else to employ in scenes where the heroine sees the hero apparently kissing the 'other woman' passionately just after she feels he has made some sort of declaration towards herself.

In romances, which are basically stories of feeling and emotion, the obstacles which keep heroine from hero for two hundred or so pages are generally, as we have already seen, of misunderstanding – the hurt to her pride that she would die rather than admit, the wrong conclusion drawn which sends him tearing off in a frenzy of jealousy because he thinks he has lost her. Supporting characters are often the means by which these misunderstandings can be brought about.

Other characters who are popular with writers and readers of romance are the heroine's rather eccentric family – possibly complete with younger brother and sister – which may on occasion be replaced by an elderly aunt instead of parents. It used to be common for heroines to be orphans, as this avoided having to explain where their parents were and why they were living alone in fierce but penniless independence in a bed-sit in London, trying to cling to a typing job for a ghastly employer and refusing to give way to the temptation to accept the hero's offer of a summer at his villa in Tuscany.

Relatives can often prove an encumbrance which a writer finds difficult to deal with, so choose any relatives you may give your heroine – or your hero – with care.

GENERAL HINTS

In romances, there is usually a very definite sense of background and you do need to be able to put the setting of your story across with complete authority. Exotic locations like the Greek islands or other sun-drenched locales are very popular, and they give readers a chance to escape mentally from the less picture-postcardy atmosphere of their home towns to the warmth of tropical beaches and the caress of balmy breezes in the palms. But you can just as easily set your story somewhere in the British Isles – Scotland or the Yorkshire Dales are quite often used – so long as you can put across a sense of place with such conviction that readers will believe the area is lovely even if it is raining.

Sensation is very important in a romance. Readers like to be told such things as what the heroine's silk dress felt like; what the freshly baked scones piled high with cream tasted like; how cool the April showers were on the heroine's flushed cheeks; how pungent the lavender in the herb garden smelled. You also give readers a sense of security if your story is firmly tied to some particular place, even if it is the sort of place they are never likely to live in.

Read as many romances as possible, examine their composition and how the author has dealt with bringing freshness to the 'formula', note what elements of 'the mixture as before' have been used. And most importantly, believe in what you write. The commonly held theory that anyone can throw a romance together with their tongue in their cheek is quite wrong.

Romance readers are quick to spot condescension or insincerity. While you are writing a romance, you too must agonise with your heroine and believe with her that one day she will find her own true love. You too have to value fidelity and possess the ability to trust; you have to leave cynicism right outside the door – at least until you have finished the 'happy ending' and completed your book.

One point about romances is that the names of the characters often follow trends of which you should be aware, though the titles are generally even less remarkable than the titles of ordinary novels. If you wrote a romance and called it *From an Enchanter Fleeing* (a quote, of course, from Shelley's 'Ode to the West Wind'), you would probably find that the publishers did not approve at all. They might suggest something much more prosaic like *Master of the Isle* or *Spellbound*. Titles of romances in general are simple, straightforward, have no suspiciously literary connotations that might confound the readers, and hint at little more than that a man and a woman are involved and that their relationship is stormy/passionate/one of attraction/one of revulsion.

The opportunities that are available with regard to the names of the hero and heroine, however, more than compensate for a lack of scope over your title. Names of romantic heroines have in recent years passed from comparatively ordinary ones like Lauri, Roslyn, Lucinda, Gina, Miranda, Brooke, Alisa, Linsie, Jonnet, Isa, Steve and Kirsty (all from the late sixties or early seventies) to more extravagant ones along the lines of Chondra, Cressida Katya, Jolian, Jade, Marichelle, Jolivette, Torey, Wallis and Vashti – to name just a few.

Amazing though it may seem, these characters are generally just ordinary working girls, doing their best in whatever their chosen lifestyle or career happens to be. But the taste of romance-goers seems to require that even if the heroine is not now blessed with flawless beauty (and sometimes even if she is), she must have a lovely or otherwise distinctive name. Jane or Ann would probably find it difficult to rate as romantic heroines these days.

The heroes too are immediately recognisable as soon as they appear on the scene, and not only because of their good looks, Italian shoes, silk handkerchief, ties and shirts. Who else but a hero would be called Gaspard, Struan, Gyles, Dom Manoel, Don Ramon, Luque, Clay, Keane, Worth, Kingston or Zan? Get to know the trends in romantic names, if you want to write this type of novel, so that you will not let the side down by christening your own hero-type something inadequate like Stan. It is more important than ever in a romance that the names should be right.

23
WAY OUT WEST

THE most easy-to-categorise 'formula' novels, apart from romances, are westerns. Like romance, the typical western has its own rules and codes of behaviour, and readers have certain requirements that have to be met.

But not all books about the American west and the opening up of new territories in the last century, can strictly be classed as 'westerns'. The average western is a plain tale with a straight storyline, and usually involves a main character who is an honest working man – often a marshal or other person of responsibility in a frontier town – in some sort of struggle with lawlessness or physical wrongdoing such as cattle-rustling, land-grabbing or intimidation.

Immense casts of characters and a deeper coverage of the subject matter than can be included in a relatively simple story automatically lift a novel out of the category of 'western'. Edna Ferber's classic of the opening up of Oklahoma territory in the 1890s, *Cimarron*, is not a western, and neither is Frank Yerby's *Western*, in spite of its title and the fact that it deals with all the drama and conflict of raw life as it was lived in the west.

Anya Seton wrote a sensitive study of a new bride's attempts to adjust to existence in an Arizona mining town – and touched on other problems such as those of Indian-White descent – in her novel *Foxfire*, but it is not a western either. The western is limited in its scope, deals only with adventure and physical action in the main, and is always told from a male point of view.

Though it presents a romanticised view of life in the west and a romanticised picture of the lives of cowboys, lawmen and other popular heroes, the western does not usually include much romance in the form of love interest.

Women play a relatively minor role, though you should read as many westerns as possible in order to familiarise yourself with the attitude of the western writer (and reader) towards the female sex.

Realistically speaking, women in pioneer days were necessary as a labour force to work alongside their men. Strength and good health and the ability to raise sons were considered of far greater importance than beauty, sexual attraction or cultural accomplishments like musical skill or literary ability. But if the men expected a great deal from their women, they provided them, in return, with an unfailing chivalry and unswerving protectiveness. In relative terms, however, women were chattels in the male-orientated world of the west, and are generally dismissed in westerns as of little importance in the real scheme of things.

If you aspire to write this type of book, your main requirement is to realise that westerns are historical novels and therefore need researching. And just because you only intend to tackle a simple, straightforward story of a man trying to make his spread pay its way, say, without any history in it, this does not mean you can skimp on the research. Everything you mention must be correct, including small facts that will make your readers feel you are speaking with the authority mentioned earlier in this book, that you *know* what you are talking about. Readers of westerns are great experts on authenticity, and will spot an error with sharper vision than any publisher's reader.

If you are going to mention specific historical facts, though – that troops were sent from one of the forts, for instance – make quite certain that the fort in question existed at that time and would have been able to supply troops when your story was taking place. And of course, if you are intending to involve any Indians, you must be familiar with whatever peaceful or warlike situations then existed between Indians and Whites, or between the different tribes. Also be aware of any incidents which might have taken place at the time of which you are writing, and which your characters would be sure to comment on.

This is only the tip of the iceberg. Western enthusiasts need to live their subject so that they eat, sleep and breathe the atmosphere of the west. Research for a western involves not only historical fact but the clothes the cowboys wore, the horses they rode and particularly the weapons they carried. Be certain you can write of guns with complete authority. You will need to be able to put the period across in every respect in order to convince addicts of westerns that you are up to scratch, as well as spinning them a good story.

24
DETECTIVE STORIES

OTHERWISE referred to as 'crime novels', detective stories have been with us for a long time. In the days when Edgar Wallace and John Creasey were busily churning forth their immense outputs, the detective story usually involved some complicated and impossible-to-solve crime like the *Locked Room* or the *Twisted Candlestick*. It generally concerned a police officer (usually an inspector) who appeared in every case with the might of the law behind him, or else a private detective who went his own way and often crossed swords with members of the Force.

Sometimes, as in the cases of the *Toff* (Creasey) or Leslie Charteris' *The Saint*, the private eye is a member of the idle rich who decided to take up detecting from philanthropic motives.

It has always been traditional that a crime writer's central character – whether policeman or private eye – must be eccentric. Dorothy L. Sayers' Lord Peter Wimsey might have come from the pages of a Wodehouse novel; Hercule Poirot is unmistakable with his egg-shaped head and luxuriant moustaches; even G. K. Chesterton's *Father Brown* is a highly unlikely crime-buster; while the number of inscrutable Oriental 'tecs who baffled readers in the twenties and thirties was proof of their popularity as examples of colourful and interesting characters.

From America came the traditional American private eye, notably as represented in the writing of Dashiel Hammett and Raymond Chandler. Another popular investigator was Ellery Queen. It was not so common to have a cop as the hero of an American crime novel, but in recent years, Lawrence Sanders is one eminent novelist who has created an impressive and convincing hero in his former chief of detectives, Edward X. Delaney.

If you want to write a crime novel today, therefore, you have the choice of the various traditional forms – the English police investigation with your hero probably being an inspector; the English crime/mystery with a private detective who works apart from the police; the American private eye in the Philip Marlowe mould; the American police investigation with a main character who is in some way connected with the police.

Or else you can create some new or original form of detective story which will give your novel a twist. One of the most noted in the past was Agatha Christie's *Ten Little Indians*, in which all the characters in turn were murdered while marooned on an island, leaving no survivor – so who had actually been responsible for the murders?

Another fairly common way of breaking loose from tradition is to make your main character an ordinary person who, for some reason or other, decides to take affairs into his or her own hands and administer private justice. Those cases where warnings of reprisals if the police should be informed make it essential for the hero or heroine to act without the assistance of the law, usually involve either kidnapping or blackmail. But though this sort of story can work, it is never very realistic if the police are left out altogether. Stories of lone 'investigators' for the government or for big companies who suspect espionage, or agents involved in some sort of spying activity, do not really come into the category of 'detective' or 'crime' fiction – these we would class as thrillers.

Any sort of action goes in a thriller, but for a crime or detective novel, it is usual for the story to be concerned specifically with a crime, which is then followed by one or more further crimes as the net closes relentlessly round the criminal. Crime stories have in recent years become much wider in their scope than the 'how-it-was-solved' case histories of the past, however. Often they explore the minds and motives of the criminal. The main characters too, who were traditionally stereotypes possessing little depth, have become real people – it is possible now for a

168

policeman or private detective to fail, make mistakes, or allow emotion to cloud his judgements.

These days, furthermore, the crime itself is often handled by the novelist with far more of a sense that this is an outrage, a violent and bloody act. In the past, private eyes wisecracked even as they gunned down a roomful of 'the ungodly'. It was like a game, and the books were written in a manner which removed them from reality completely. You could get away with this in a rather superficial sort of spy-thriller today, possibly, but not in a serious attempt at a detective or crime story. No longer is crime some sort of 'poor relation' – the genre has reached previously unthinkable heights of literary excellence with the works of writers like P. D. James and Ruth Rendell.

If you want to write crime stories, be certain you have all your facts correct, including police procedure and such minutiae as the symptoms of different poisons. The rare poison of the South American Indians, which knocks your victim for six when mysteriously aimed from the minstrel's gallery through a blow-pipe, will produce only hysterical laughter in your readers. Check on all facts – however distasteful – like how and when rigor mortis would set in, or how long the remains of the last meal eaten by the victim would remain in the stomach.

Make sure you are in full possession of all the facts you need to know, and then make sure you plan your novel with particular care. As we have already seen, the way in which clues are laid for both the detective and the readers, and the way in which the novelist allows them to become obvious, requires skilful handling. You have to do your planning in advance – the crime story cannot proceed on sudden bursts of inspiration from the author's subconscious. The framework has to be prepared, the technical tricks worked out, before the author makes any serious attempt at the opening pages.

After that, it is up to you. There has always been a huge and eager audience for crime stories – a whole literature on the psychology of crime novels and why people read them has come into existence. Apart from the psychology, though, keep your readers guessing and never let them catch up with you. Basically, Raymond Chandler had the right idea when he advised: 'When in doubt, have two guys come through the door with guns in their fists.' Well, he should know!

25
OTHER GENRES

WHILE it is true that there are other types of novel which can be described as genre books, these do not usually follow any particular formula.

Science fiction, for instance, is now more highly respected than it has possibly ever been, and has passed far beyond the 'space travel and fights with little green aliens' versions which featured so often in the past. But in order to write a science fiction novel you need more than ever to be familiar – to some degree anyway – with the enormous body of work which already exists, and to be aware of the technology as well as the imaginative scope that can smudge science fiction over into science fantasy.

The best works of science fiction – and indeed science fantasy – follow no patterns, are written to no formulae, but are rich and often immensely dignified creations in their own right. If you can write one of these books, the sky is literally your limit so far as imagination and freedom of expression goes. You will see, if you examine great writers in these fields, however, that their novels are not only unbelievably wide in physical and imaginative scope but are, compensatingly, constructed and written with all the precision of mathematics and their own technologies. The best writing by masters like Ray Bradbury and Ursula le Guin will teach you more than any book on 'How To'.

Another genre into which books can be classified, but which is difficult to define before the story is actually written, is horror. Again, horror stories are published which turn out to be something utterly different from any concept readers might previously have had of what a horror story should be like.

In the past, horror was of the gothic variety, in the

Edgar Allan Poe style, with dark brooding melancholy, coffins and bodies, swirling fog and cobwebs and unaccountable sounds in the night. Writers like Shirley Jackson, with her superb *The Haunting of Hill House*, brought horror bang up to date, right into the homes and cars and lives and minds of ordinary people in ordinary situations *now*.

Studying novels by current popular horror writers like Stephen King, Peter Straub and James Herbert will reveal that apart from the ability to chill their readers, they do not write to any formula. Their books can be about anything – and so can yours.

One type of novel which does almost have a formula to it, in the same way as a romance or a western, is the 'saga'. These are usually extremely long historical novels, which either cover the fortunes of one strong-willed character – generally a woman – as she rises from the depths of deprivation and poverty to immense power and influence, or else deal with several generations in a family which has some connection with, usually, industry – steel or the wool trade, or the railways. This type of family saga generally chronicles how the family started off in industry when some enterprising member saw the potential in railways/wool/iron or whatever, during the late 1700s or early 1800s. The drama is provided by the squabbles and feuds, rises and falls in family and personal fortunes, births, loves and deaths of various members down a generation or two.

The saga can be brought up to date, and need not be historical, so long as it is similarly concerned with a background of one particular industrial or other empire, and the in-fighting as your heroine scratches her wild-cat way to the top, loving and hating some lusciously attractive males on the way. The shelves of most bookshops are crammed with this type of novel, if you want to study the genre.

One last point which should be made is that in recent years there has been an emergence of what can loosely be described as 'woman's fiction', incorporating many viewpoints and issues which were not generally acceptable to publishers or the reading public in the past.

The society of today is not only freeing itself – and finding that sexual and other freedom carries with it bonds of its own and unsuspected problems both physical and psychological – but is increasingly aware that never before has it amalgamated so many races, so many creeds, so many different cultures. New genres, new types of novels, will increasingly appear as the demands of tomorrow are met by discerning novelists. These questions have never required answering in the past, never needed clarification or exploration. The prospect is a thrilling one. Writers in these fields are the pioneers, the explorers who will point the way for the generations to come.

PART V
WHAT MAKES
A BEST-SELLER?

WHAT MAKES
A BEST SELLER?

FIRST let us examine just what we mean by the term 'best-seller'. When it was first coined, a 'best-seller' meant a book which had sold in large numbers because it was unexpected, different; because it was something that was *not* written to any formula and it was unlike other books. Such novels created new trends, set new fashions and had the reading public anxious not to miss out on something that was being talked about by everyone else.

But over the years, a 'best-seller' has come to mean any book, whether the author is known or not, and whether there have been others like it previously or not, which sells a large number of copies. In this case, what makes it a 'best-seller' is often the fact that the author is a name with which even the most un-literary members of the public are familiar because of massive promotion in the media (I need not mention names of novelists who come into this category), or that the author has written other novels which have been best-sellers and has a large following of readers who will buy every new book he or she might write. Popular authors in this second category include Catherine Cookson, Lena Kennedy, Virginia Andrews, Wilbur Smith, Dick Francis. Such writers sell on their previous reputation for quality and excellence in their own spheres.

As a new writer, you cannot hope to compete here, of course. No publisher is going to risk a million-dollar promotional campaign on a book without some sort of guarantee that within weeks the author's name will be a household word. And neither can you cash in on a previously achieved reputation. Even quite successful writers find it difficult to establish followings of readers substantial enough to ensure that when a new novel with their name on it appears, the public will flock into bookshops in large numbers and buy copies.

I am a reasonably successful novelist, for instance, and thousands of people – literally – read various editions of my novels every year, but my name is relatively unknown to the public at large. Most other moderately successful novelists who are not one of the 'big few' are in the same position.

So how else can we determine what makes a 'best-seller' so that we can – hopefully – write one? If we put on one side the promotional aspect of bringing out a new book – the efforts made by publishers to push their product at the public – we will find that the books which become the real best-sellers, the ones which I have already mentioned as setting trends and starting new fashions, can rarely be predicted. It is their unexpectedness, their freshness, their original outlook which breaks the mould of established literary form and seizes the imagination of the public.

Often the books which become overnight best-sellers do not last for very long. They may have a certain novelty value, but they are not substantial enough to survive as great work, classics of tomorrow. In recent years, there have been novels which had clues in them to hidden treasure – Kit Williams's *Masquerade*, for instance, which was immensely successful a few years ago, but which has been all but forgotten now.

Another best-seller of novelty value was a facsimile of a handwritten manuscript, supposedly the diary of a woman trying to survive with her companions in a fall-out shelter after a nuclear attack. This was reproduced as though it was an actual copy of her diary, and even the cover bore no author's or publisher's name so far as I can recall, but said simply *Jenny's Diary*.

If you can come up with some extremely novel idea such as the two I have detailed, you might be able to interest a publisher, but it would have to be something very special.

On the whole, publishers are not particularly fond of new ideas, and the entire history of best-sellers is cluttered with tales of immense successes which were almost refused – or which actually were refused – by publishers who swore the idea was hopeless. Erich Segal's *Love Story* was emphatically rejected at first, even though he was already an established name. It just won't work, the publishers declared – until he proved them wrong.

In many ways, the 'best-seller list' is a hit-and-miss affair. In the end it is the public, the readers, who make the decisions. It is they who choose the novels which become best-sellers, and they often do it without the assistance of the critics or the publishers. They begin to talk to each other about some great new book; they begin to ask for it in libraries; they tell friends, who read it and tell their friends. Genuine enthusiasm like this for any author or any book is worth more than all the promotional campaigns in the world.

The qualities of books which become best-sellers are that, apart from seizing the imagination of the public, they voice some previously unspoken popular concern or express feelings which are running underground, as it were, at that period in time. When James Hilton's *Lost Horizon* appeared in the thirties, it epitomised something people everywhere felt they were searching for - their own Shangri-la, the land where time stands still and there is no war and all men are brothers living in harmony and wisdom.

This ideal was underlined by Orson Welles, who commented: 'Almost all serious stories in the world are stories of a failure with a death in it. But there is more lost paradise in them than defeat. To me that's the central theme of Western culture; the lost paradise.'

In the fifties, best-sellers took a new turn. Alan Sillitoe's *Saturday Night and Sunday Morning* and *The Loneliness of the Long Distance Runner* were only two titles that turned the spotlight onto a previously ignored section of the community – the provincial working classes – and presented them in a relatively realistic and sympathetic

179

manner. The reason why such novels were successful was because there was a demand for them at that time – in the social revolution of the fifties and sixties, the concept that literature was only for the upper crust was being determinedly overthrown.

Angry Young Men everywhere – not only in the theatre, where they identified wholeheartedly with John Osborne's *Look Back in Anger* – wanted to hear about *their* particular lifestyles, *their* particular problems. And readers who were neither angry, young nor men, were thrilled and fascinated at the glimpses revealed of rugged and by no means moral goings-on in comparatively sordid settings.

To be a best-seller, a book has to be in the right place at the right time, which is often purely a matter of luck. And once one book has caught the public imagination, there follows a spate of similar novels, all of which have really missed the boat, since by the time the first book has appeared and the writers who decide to cash in on the trend have written theirs – even if they manage to place it with a publisher – at least a year will have passed and it will take a further year for their own book to go through the production process. Thus several years might have gone by before the second book appeared, by which time the public could well have lost interest in that particular type of novel.

The most we can really say is that a potential best-seller has to be good, it has to be original and different and it has to reflect – in some way or another – the prevailing mood or popular thought of that moment. This is a set of requirements which are extremely difficult to follow. Jeffrey Archer, it is claimed, set out to recover his fortunes by writing a 'best-seller', and in spite of living a very full life, proceeded to produce not only one but a string of them.

These, though, were not books which burst – in the manner I have described – on the public and seized their imagination. They sold partly on the author's name and partly on the interesting background and subject matter. How do 'best-sellers' of this sort measure up against the advice given by Samuel Butler?

When a man is in doubt about this or that in his writing it will often guide him if he asks himself how it will tell a hundred years hence.

The really successful best-sellers are those which, in a hundred years, may seem dated, but will not be so dated as to prove embarrassing. In the 2000's, people will be able to read Richard Llewellyn's *How Green was my Valley*, Cronin's *The Citadel*, Sergeanne Golon's popular historical series which began with *Angelique*, Rumer Godden's *The Greengage Summer*, John Braine's *Room at the Top*, Kingsley Amis's *Lucky Jim* – to name just a few – and find that, in spite of the fact that they are obviously 'period pieces' in the same way that the works of Dickens, Thackeray and George Eliot are 'period pieces', there is some underlying richness, some seam of gold, which means that (in a lesser manner possibly than the greats) these are books that can stand the test of time.

The authors who produce best-sellers might well have no idea of what they are doing. If they studied the lists of publishers, aimed at a target section of the populace, tried to produce a manuscript which would comply with all the current requirements for novels, they would never write books like *Watership Down* (Richard Adams' novel about rabbits) or *Jonathan Livingston Seagull*.

Paul Gallico went even further than birds and animals with his *Snowflake*! But the readers of the fifties lapped it up.

So it is the fact that so many novelists are unaware of any need to conform, or else decide they do not want to conform, which – one way or another – means that books continue to be produced which are utterly unlike any other books and do not fit into any recognised category. Most of these are unlikely to be best-sellers. But somewhere, some new writer may quite unconsciously be struggling with the novel that will be on every bookstall this time next year, selling in tens of thousands because it expresses what is in the secret heart of every reader and speaks in the voice of the people *now*.

It may appear that certain names have been omitted from this resume which should automatically have been mentioned. What about the novels by people of the quality of Graham Greene, Nevil Shute, George Orwell, Doris Lessing, Pamela Frankau? Not to mention greats of the stature of Hemingway, Virginia Woolf, Evelyn Waugh, E.M. Forster?

In fact, great literature seldom achieves the distinction of becoming a popular *best-seller* unless it is through a side-effect like the fact that a film of the book has been released. John Fowles became the best-selling author of *The French Lieutenant's Woman* but *after* the public had thrilled to Meryl Streep and Jeremy Irons on the screen. And people who had never heard of Paul Scott suddenly became devotees of his work after the TV serial *Jewel in the Crown* had held huge audiences spellbound week after week.

Other ways in which 'literary' novels can become best-sellers is through what we might describe as their 'notoriety value'. It was generally recognised, for instance, that the novels of D. H. Lawrence were interesting and made a valuable contribution to literature, but the name of D. H. Lawrence was not one which rang in the ears of the masses and sent them scurrying to buy up copies – until *Lady Chatterley's Lover* was put on trial! The thought of exactly how scandalous this novel might actually be prompted the public to purchase copies like hot cakes as soon as they were available and it became a best-seller, but not because of its undoubted beauty as a piece of writing.

More recently, the outrage surrounding the writer Salman Rushdie and his book *The Satanic Verses* has made this an overwhelming best-seller, yet it is more than likely that sheer curiosity prompted many sales, and that a large percentage of the people who bought the novel had no real intention of sitting down with it for a good read.

Winners of literary prizes, writers whose work is intensely cerebral, or even those whose novels are elegant and literate but have no particular popular appeal, rarely become best-sellers. They are in a class of their own – their

182

writing is timeless, they often produce small masterpieces to be appreciated like exquisite jewels, by the few.

It is rare that a writer can combine quality and literary elegance with popular appeal. One author who has done this is Anita Brookner. But by and large, the best-seller is always that little bit louder, bigger, more emotive, more colourful, more garish than the literary novel. The public enjoys the fact that there are best-sellers, often (in a perverse manner) because it can allow itself the pleasure of pulling them to pieces. If they did not exist, publishers would have to invent them and invent the authors who are notorious for writing them, especially those super-sellers whom the public love to hate.

Robert Benchley, the eminent American humorist, probably expressed a view which many authors of best-sellers would echo if they were honest enough: 'It took me fifteen years to discover that I had no talent for writing, but I couldn't give it up because by that time I was too famous!'

PART VI
AUTHOR'S NOTE

AUTHOR'S NOTE

IF a Martian or creature from some other galaxy landed on Earth and, in the course of its investigations into human culture, tried to discover why people wrote novels, it would be very hard put to find an answer.

In spite of Samuel Johnson's declaration that: 'No man but a blockhead ever wrote, except for money', there is overwhelming evidence that at any given moment, hundreds – probably thousands – of would-be authors are working on their novels without any promise of payment to spur them forward. Many are aware that they might not sell this particular book, but as one lady who has been writing for a year remarked to me: 'Oh, I'm just doing this one as practice!'

So if it is not the prospect of large cheques arriving to boost their bank accounts, nor the thought – which most writers are realistic enough to recognise as just a pipe dream – of instant and overwhelming fame once their book is published, why do they do it?

If our visiting Martian had studiously perused the contents of this book, it would, I hope, have been made very clear to him that the popular belief that the novelist's job is some sort of sinecure, where days and nights are spent in riotous living while the novels write themselves in some mysterious fashion, is utterly misplaced.

He would have seen that there is a great deal of hard work involved, sheer slogging and mental labour, sustained effort and tremendous endurance – all far beyond what any reputable employer could reasonably ask of his employees, even though they are paid for the work they do. But the novelist has no guarantee whatsoever that he will receive even a kindly word, far less an acceptance.

So why do people write novels? Why have I devoted the greater part of my life to novel-writing? Why are you reading this book, in between working on your own pile of ever-increasing chapters, and aspiring to become a novelist?

It is often declared that writers, as well as painters, musicians, ballet dancers and even nuns – anyone who has a vocation – are born and not made. People do not ask to be novelists; they have no choice. They feel while they are writing their novel that it would not matter if there was a tidal wave down the High Street, a volcano erupting round the corner, and World War III had just been declared, so long as they were left in peace and quiet to plough on to the end. Life itself, the raw material of the novelist's art, is to him less substantial and of less importance than what he feels he must create.

In his own way, the novelist is a god. He creates the world in which his characters move and have their being; he manipulates their lives and their deaths, he wields absolute power. When the novelist is writing he reaches into dimensions of which non-artistic souls can gain only the vaguest glimpse. When the novelist is writing, he makes his mark upon history, plants his footsteps (in the words of Longfellow) on the sands of time.

Perhaps the mark on history will prove so faint as to be non-existent; perhaps the footsteps in those eternal sands will get swept away by the tide of reality when the novelist discovers that nobody is interested in his book and it is relegated eventually to the back of the attic, where it gathers dust and is gradually nibbled to pieces by resident mice.

But this is why people write novels. They have something to say to the world, something to give. Into every writer's novel goes a part of himself. Derision, mockery, misunderstanding will not harm the novel, but can cut the novelist to the heart. Emily Bronte died of it when *Wuthering Heights* was damned by the critics.

We all have dreams, however reluctant we are to

acknowledge them, of reaching the stars, of somehow achieving something greater than we are. All good writers know this and, however cynical they might be in everyday life, they will not deny the truth.

The screenwriter Ben Hecht commented:

Writing cheaply, writing falsely, writing with 'less' than you have, is a painful thing. To betray belief is to feel sinful, guilty – and taste bad.

William Faulkner put it this way:

The writer's only responsibility is to his art. He will be completely ruthless if he is a good one. He has a dream. It anguishes him so much that he must get rid of it. He has no peace until then... If a writer has to rob his mother, he will not hesitate; the *Ode to a Grecian Urn* is worth any number of old ladies.

'Genius', said Edward Bulwer, Earl of Lytton, 'does what it must, and Talent does what it can'.

And so, we write.